HAIKU MASTER
TAIGI

TAIGI TAN

TRANSLATED BY
EARL TROTTER

Peach Blossom Press

Peach Blossom Press
Chatham, ON

Cover: Portrait of Taigi from 不夜菴太祇發句集 (1772). Waseda University, call number: 文庫 31 A0468.

Taigi Tan (1709–1771)
  Haiku Master Taigi
  Translated by Earl Trotter

  ISBN 978-1-7387466-1-3

1. Taigi Tan (1709-1771).   2. Japanese Haiku.

for 藤井 由紀子

CONTENTS

INTRODUCTION

History of Haiku

Before beginning the discussion, note that the use of "syllable" here is a little different from the usage for English. It could be rendered as "unit of sound." The difference is that, in Japanese, long vowels and double consonants count as 2 syllables and the "n" after a vowel, one. So in romaji "*nan*" is two syllables as is "*shii*" while "*kakko*" is three syllables. Note that the long "e" and long "o" are usually rendered "ei" and "ou" (there are exceptions). The long syllables can also be written with a macron, e.g. "*shī*." As well, "lines" are not lines as in English verse but represent the five or seven (or other) syllabic unit. Japanese verse was traditionally written vertically with no breaks.

The roots of haiku go back to the beginning of Japanese poetry. All the ancient forms consist of five or seven syllables. There were four main types. First there is the *kauta,* in a question and answer format consisting of three lines with the syllabic pattern, 5-7-7. Related is the *sedouka*, basically a double *kauta*. The *chouka* are built of alternating lines of five and seven syllables to an indeterminate length, concluding with a seven-syllable line. Within the *chouka*, there might be a break in the pattern with consecutive five or seven syllable lines. These forms eventually fell out of use although the *chouka* was a prominent form in the Manyoshu (compiled after 759).

Of greater importance are waka (or tanka). It consists of five lines with a syllabic pattern of 5-7-5-7-7. Initially this tended to consist of two couplets and a last line refrain. Later new breakdowns emerged in a 5-7-5 7-7 split where the first three lines modified the last two or where the two parts were related but

1

independent grammatically. Overtime there was also a growing use of a pause after the first line. This gives the first three lines a haiku flavour. By the time of the Kokinshu, compiled in 905, waka was the predominant form. A final point to notice was that the imperial anthologies of waka, over hundreds of years, divided the poems in sections and the four seasons were given prominence.

Beginning in early Heian, there appeared some waka where one person would compose the first three lines and another person, the last two. Such are called renga, or linked verse. This was mainly an exercise in wit. However the practice continued and slowly developed. Verses began to become linked – one writer composing a 5-7-5 opening then another adding 7-7, then 5-7-5 and so on. Eventually one hundred links became the standard. The first five lines would have a certain meaning, but lines four to eight would change the core idea, then lines six to ten likewise. By 1200 renga was a distinct genre. A group of poets would meet and then compose spontaneously to the preceding verse. Renga developed very complex rules for linking and also developed season words, or *kigo,* to be followed. The opening three lines were deemed very important and called *hokku. Hokku* were sometimes published separately and this gave them their own identity.

From renga, a humorous form developed, *haikai no renga,* which we will hereafter refer simply as *haikai.* The opening verse, as in renga, is called *hokku.* In addition to humour and wit, it also employed more colloquial language. Renga had followed the diction of traditional waka poets. The change here can also be traced to a shift where the merchant class became more involved in poetry. In Heian times it was limited to aristocrats. The first school of haikai was the Teimon School founded by Teitoku (1570-1653). Basically their principles were identical to renga, with most of its complex rules intact, with the exception of the use of colloquial language.

A reaction set in against the complexities of the Teimon School and Soin (1604-1682) founded the Danrin School. This school sought freedom and almost any diction and subject matter, including vulgar language and obscenities, were used. There was a heated competition between the two schools. Through all this development was the increasing focus on the independent *hokku.*

Although a later appellation (see below), we will refer to the independent *hokku* as haiku henceforth given it ubiquitous use.

The course of haiku was changed forever with the appearance of Matsuo Basho (1644–1694). He promoted the use of ordinary language as means of sincere expression. As well, subject matter was broadened from the Teimon School, along with humour, but not to the excesses of the Danrin School. Basho promoted a series of various approaches to *haiku* – in fact, not staying put in one theory was part of his aesthetic. He talked of sincerity (*makoto*) and later lightness (*karumi*) and his poems often exhibited *sabi* and *wabi* – feelings of transience, imperfection, poverty and simplicity. Basho had many disciples, the major being Takarai Kikaku who wrote a moving account of Basho's last days and was influential until the time of Buson.

Basho was based in Edo. In the Kansai region (Kyoto, Osaka), Uejima Onitsura (1661–1738 wrote a poetics of haiku based on sincerity (*makoto*). His and Basho's ideas are likely connected in some manner, if only through Onitsura's contacts with Basho's disciples.

The two major haiku poets after Basho were Yosa Buson (1716–1784) and Kobayashi Issa (1763–1828). Buson was a poet known for his sensibility and lyricism. He sought to be natural, not encumbered by too many rules. In his lifetime he was more renown for his paintings and he is considered a master of *haiga,* a form of painting incorporating haiku aesthetics tending to a simple (though not simplistic) style. Issa, who was not well known in his lifetime is the foremost poet of humanity imbued with an atmosphere of pathos. There is also much down-to-earth humour in many of his haiku. Tan Taigi (1709-1771), a contemporary of Buson we deal with below. The finest woman haiku poet is considered to be Chiyo-ni (Kaga no Chiyo) (1703-1775).

The bridge to the modern era came with Masaoka Shiki (1867–1902). Considered one of the four great haiku poets, along with Basho, Buson and Issa, Shiki was the one to designate what had been known as *hokku*, as haiku. He favoured haiku based on a realistic observation of nature. Shiki revivified the haiku form. It has not only been exceedingly popular in Japan since his death but enjoys a popularity worldwide.

3

Characteristics of Haiku

Haiku can be succinctly summarized as a Japanese poetic form consisting of seventeen syllables in a 5-7-5 format, which will include a season word (*kigo*) and a "cutting word" (*kireji*). As mentioned previously, the syllable is a "sound unit" and the 5-7-5 format, rendered in lines, in English, is not done so in Japanese. The haiku topic will be on a seasonal event, whether pertaining to nature or a social occasion. Haiku is usually in two parts, either the first line versus the last two, or first two lines versus the last. The cutting word often serves to build this structure (end of line one, two, or three) and as well frequently highlights the preceding phrase (like an exclamation mark).

Since Basho and Onitsura, haiku has been seen as representing the true feelings and/or experience of the poet. However, this should not be seen as being solely a spontaneous insight into life or nature, immediately rendered down as haiku (the Zen moment). Haiku, even of masters such as Basho, are constantly revised in composition and certain events are, in fact, imaginary (viz. certain episodes in Basho's *The Narrow Road to the Deep North*). However, the best haiku will certainly be insightful and represent the poet's true feelings, an aesthetic that goes back to the earliest writings of Chinese and Japanese aesthetics (see the Mao Commentary to the *Book of Songs* and the *Preface* to the *Kokinshu*).

Tan Taigi (炭太祇)

Taigi was born in 1709 in Edo (Tokyo). He studied haiku under Suitoku then Keikitsu. He travelled about the country in 1751, including Kyushu. He ended up in Kyoto the same year and became a Zen priest. He lived in Shinjuan at Daitokuji where the famous priest, Ikkyu, had had a hermitage. However, he soon left and went to live in Kyoto's red-light district, Shimabara, to be near his friend and patron (and brothel owner), Donshi. He made friends with many kabuki actors (he had done likewise in Edo) and taught haiku and calligraphy to them as well as courtesans. He was involved in haiku circles and became friends with Yosa Buson. The pleasure district was also known as the nightless city and copying this Taigi called his haiku school and home the nightless hermitage (不夜庵 fuya'an). He lived in Shimabara for the rest of his life but made periodic visits to Edo. He died in 1771 reportedly from a brain hemorrhage brought on from overdrinking.

Along with Buson he sought a return to the values of Basho. Taigi could present a simple human situation or reflect the grandeur of nature. Blyth felt Taigi was a near equal to the four masters: Basho, Buson, Issa and Shiki. Blyth's final comments on Taigi are worth repeating: "The greatness of Taigi is connected with his realisation that haiku is not religion, as with Basho; it is not art, as Buson thought; it is not Issa's consolation for the tragic irony of life; haiku is, or should be, life itself, no more, no less.[1]"

The Translation

The translation of the haiku is fairly literal. I have tried to follow the original images sequentially but with Japanese this is not always feasible. The important point is to make the key image clearly stand out. The form is reflected in the three-line structure but no attempt has been made for a consistent number of syllables or accents per line. The Japanese text is from various sources on the internet including university archives but a few were transcribed from Blyth. Haiku from different sources matched, other than the use of kanji versus hiragana in some instances. Some 740 haiku have been translated. The haiku are arranged by, but not within, season. There is often ambiguity in the pieces and alternative renderings are possible in some instances

Most of my sources had no romaji, so although overwhelmingly correct, the renderings should be considered provisional. I have replaced the sound of the older forms, は (ha), へ (he), ひ (hi), and

---

[1]   R. H. Blyth, *A History of Haiku* Vol.1, p. 308.

ふ (fu), where applicable, as they are now, in many instances, わ (wa), え (e), い (i), and う (u). The archaic ゐ (wi) is i in modern Japanese. Note that ふ (fu) was often used as a verb ending where う (u) is now employed. There are also the following older stand-alone forms that are retained in modern Japanese but have a different sound: は (ha), へ (he) and を (wo) as wa (topic marker), e (to) and o (object marker) respectively. As well, the pre-modern rendering of "today" as けふ (kefu) has been replaced by kyou in the romaji. The odd other item has been modernized.

Further Reading

There is virtually nothing in English on Taigi. The six Blyth volumes have many haiku by Taigi scattered throughout their pages. There is a chapter in *A History of Haiku*, Vol. 1 (pp. 289-308) that deals specifically with Taigi and is highly recommended (as are all of Blyth's works on haiku). Of course there are other scattered translations in various haiku anthologies and on the web.

The other entries for further reading relate to haiku in general and to the four most noted poets, Basho, Buson, Issa and Shiki. Yasuda's volume was of great help in doing the Introduction. As well, Lanoue's website of Issa translations was useful in resolving certain ambiguities in the text where the same term was used by both Taigi and Issa. Of course, this list is just a fraction of the works available.

Blyth, R. H. *Haiku*. 4 Vols. Tokyo: The Hokuseido Press, 1949–1952.

_____. *A History of Haiku*. 2 Vols. Tokyo: The Hokuseido Press, 1963–1964.

Henderson, Harold G. *An Introduction to Haiku*. Garden City, New York: Doubleday Anchor Books, 1958.

Higginson, William J. *The Haiku Handbook*. New York: McGraw-Hill Book Company, 1985.

Lanoue, David. *Haiku of Kobayashi Issa*. http://haikuguy.com/issa/

Masaoka Shiki. *Selected Poems*. Translated by Burton Watson. New York: Columbia University Press, 1997.

Matsuo Basho. *Basho's Haiku*. 2 Vols. Translated by Toshiharu Oseko. Saitama: Toshiharu Oseko, 1990-1996.

_____. *The Complete Haiku*. Translated by Jane Reichhold. Tokyo: Kodansha International Ltd., 2008.

McElligot, Patrick. (1970). *The Life and Work of Kobayashi Issa*. Doctoral Dissertation at the School of Oriental and African Studies, London. ProQuest Dissertations Publishing.

Sawa, Yuki, & Shiffert, Edith. *Haiku Master Buson*. San Francisco: Heian International Publishing Company, 1978.

Yasuda, Kenneth. *The Japanese Haiku*. Boston: Tuttle Publishing, 1957.

New Year

あら手きて羽子つき上し軒端かな

ara te kite hago tsuki ue shi nokiba kana

Ah, the hand approaches!
　　The shuttlecock reaches
　　　　the top of the eaves.

初寅や頼光しばし市原野

hatsutora ya yorimitsu shibashi ichiharano

First Day of the Tiger!
　　Yorimitsu out for a while
　　　　at Ichiharano[2].

鉢の子に粥たく庵も若なかな

hachi no ko ni kayu taku io mo wakana kana

Cooking rice gruel in the child's pot
　　at my hut –
　　　　the fresh spring greens![3]

---

[2]　There are many allusions in this haiku. On the First Day of the Tiger in the New Year, Bishamon was worshipped at Kuramadera Temple (and elsewhere) which is near Ichiharano, now a part of Kyoto. At this place Minamoto no Yorimitsu (948–1021), on his way to Kuramadera, was attacked by Kidomaru, an oni (demon). Kudomaru was killed (see *Koko Chumin Ju*).

[3]　Seven different herbs were picked on the 6th day of New Year's for making rice cakes (mochi) and rice gruel, eaten the next day.

穴一の筋引すてつ梅が下

ana ichi no sujibiki sutetsu ume ga shita

"One Hole[4]" –
giving up drawing the line
under the plum blossoms!

万歳のゑぼし姿やわたし船

banzai no eboshi sugata ya watashi fune

The hats
of the Banzai dancers[5]
look like my boat!

小書院のこの夕ぐれや福寿草

kojoin no kono yuugure ya fukujusou

At twilight
in the small room –
pheasant's eye[6]!

---

[4] A children's New Year game similar to pitching pennies in concept but using a hole. A line was drawn about one metre from the hole to stand behind.

[5] A New Year's performance. The dancers wore a particular kind of *eboshi* hat.

[6] A member of the buttercup family.

二日には箒のさきやふく寿草

futsuka ni wa houki no saki ya fukujusou

On the second day of New Year's
   at the end of the broom –
      pheasant's eye!

七くさや兄弟の子の起そろひ

nanakusa ya kyoudai no ko no okisoroi

The seven herbs![7]
   The siblings
      all wake up together!

とりて内裏を出るや小挑灯

toshitorite dairi o deru ya kochouchin

Welcoming the New Year!
   Leaving the Imperial Palace,
      small lantern in hand.

---

[7]   Seven different herbs were picked on the 6th day of New Year's for making
      rice cakes (mochi) and rice gruel, eaten the next day.

節に成る古き訛や傀儡師

setsu ni naru furuki namari ya kairaishi

>It reaches the part
>>with the archaic language –
>>>puppeteers![8]

口馴し百や孫子の手毬うた

kuchinarashi hyaku ya magoko no temari uta

>Counting to one hundred –
>>my granddaughter's
>>>*temari* song[9]!

長閑さに無沙汰の神社回りけり

nodokasa ni busata no jinja mawari keri

>It's been a while
>>since I've visited a shrine
>>>that's tranquil![10]

---

[8] This refers to *bunraku*, Japanese puppet theatre, with its puppeteers (3 per puppet), chanter and samisen player.

[9] *Temeri* is a girl's game using a ball made of fabrics. It can be a ball game or simply bouncing the ball to a song (*uta*). This would be a counting song.

[10] This alludes to the shrines being crowded in the New Year period.

からくりの首尾のわるさよ鳳巾
karakuri no kubi o no waru sa yo hou kin

> The puppet is ripped
> from head to tail!
> The cloth phoenix.

はねつくや世ご〻ろしらぬ大またげ
hane tsuku ya yogokoro shiranu oomatage

> Playing shuttlecock!
> Striding here and there
> with nothing else on her mind.

羽つくや用意おかしき立まはり
hane tsuku ya youi okashiki tachimawari

> Playing shuttlecock!
> It's odd – getting ready to play
> she walks about.

七草や余所の聞へもあまり下手

nanakusa ya yoso no kiku e mo amari heta

> The seven herbs![11]
>> I hear of a place
>>> they inadvertently missed some.

春駒や男顔なるおゝなの子

harukoma ya otokogao naru ouna no ko

> The horse performers[12] –
>> one woman's son
>>> wears the mask of a man.

初寅や慾つらあかき山おろし

hatsutora ya yoku tsura akaki yamaoroshi

> First Day of the Tiger![13]
>> Faces look red with craving –
>>> wind blowing down the mountain.

万歳や舞おさめたるしたり顔

manzai ya maiosametaru shitarigao

Manzai dancers![14]
　　They complete their dance
　　　　with a self-satisfied look on their faces.

子を抱て御階を上る御修法哉

ko o idate mihashi o noboru mishiho kana

Holding the child,
　　climbing the stairs of the Shishinden[15] –
　　　　prayers[16] for the New Year.

鰒喰し我にもあらぬ雑煮哉

fugu kuishi ware ni mo aranu zouni kana

I'm not
　　eating blowfish[17] –
　　　　it's *mochi* soup[18].

---

[14] A group of comedic performers visiting homes and celebrating the New Year with drums, song and dance.
[15] The ceremonial hall of the Imperial Palace.
[16] This was the *mishiho*. The Shinto prayers for the emperor and nation took place on the 1st to 7th days of the first month while the Shingon Buddhist ritual took place from the 8th to 14th.
[17] One can die from improperly prepared blowfish.
[18] Rice cake soup or *zoni*.

目を明て聞て居る也四方の春

me o meite kite iru nari shihou no haru

> Looking
> > and listening –
> > > it's New Year's everywhere!

年玉や利ぬくすりの医三代

toshidama ya kikunu kusuri no i sandai

> New Year's gift!
> > The useless medicine of
> > > of a third generation doctor[19].

とし玉や杓子数添ふ草の庵

toshidama ya shakushi kazu sou kusa no io

> New Year's gift!
> > A bamboo ladle, just enough
> > > for my thatched hut.

---

[19] A common New Year's gift. Apparently a third generation doctor might be lax.

元日の居ごゝろや世にふる畳
ganjitsu no igokoro ya yo ni furudatami

    On New Year's Day
      so comfortable
        on my old tatami mat!

Spring

はるの行音や夜すがら雨のあし

haru no yuku oto ya yo sugara ame no ashi

> The sound of departing spring –
>> all night
>>> a fine drizzle.

寒食や竈をめぐるあぶら虫

kanshoku ya kamado o meguru aburamushi

> Cold Food Day![20]
>> Scurrying all over the hearth,
>>> aphids.

諸声やうき藻にまとふむら蛙

morogoe ya ukime ni matou mura kaeru

> A chorus of voices!
>> Jumbled up in the seaweed,
>>> a throng of frogs.

---

[20] Derived from the Cold Food Festival in China and originally held the 105th day after winter solstice. Not using fire was the key idea. Little remains of this event in modern Japan.

凧白し長閑過ての夕ぐもり
tako shiroshi nodoka sugite no yuugumori

White kites float
in unearthly serenity
on a cloudy evening.

蕨採て筧にあらふひとりかな
warabi seite kakei ni arau hitori kana

All alone
gathering bracken
and washing it in the trough.

膝たてゝおそき日みるや天の原
hizatatete osoki hi miru ya ama no hara

Kneeling down on a spring day
I gaze about –
the boundless heavens!

池のふねへ藤こぼるゝや此夕べ
ike no fune e fuji koboreru ya kon yuube

> This evening,
>> wisteria blossoms
>>> spill over the boat on the pond.

泊らばや遅き日の照る奥座敷
hakuraba ya osoki hi no teru oku zashiki

> Staying overnight –
>> the sun shines late
>>> into my *tatami* room[21].

堀川の畠からたつ胡蝶かな
horikawa no hatake kara tatsu kochou kana

> From the field
>> by the canal
>>> a butterfly ascends.

---

[21]   A formal Japanese room with *tatami* mats.

山路きてむかふ城下や凧の数

yamaji kite mukau jouka ya tako no kazu

Coming along the mountain road
where it faces the castle –
scores of kites.

永日やいまだ泊らぬ鶏の声

eijitsu ya imada tomaranu tori no koe

The long spring day!
They haven't roosted yet –
squawking chickens.

しなへよく畳へ置や藤の花

shina e yoku tatami e oku ya fuji no hana

Put them down carefully
on the *totami* mat –
wisteria blossoms.

半ば来て雨にぬれゐる花見哉

nakaba kite ame ni nure iru hanami kana

    Halfway there,
        I got drenched in the rain –
            cherry blossom viewing.

暮遅く日の這わたる畳かな

kure osoku hi no hawataru tatami kana

    The end of a long spring day –
        the sun creeps
            along the *tatami* mat.

遅日の光のせたり沖の浪

chijitsu no hikari nosetari oki no nami

    Reflecting the light
        of a late sunset in spring –
            the waves offshore.

狂言は南無ともいはず壬生念仏

kyougen wa namu tomo iwazu mibu nenbutsu

> Kyogen[22].
>> "Hail" not said together –
>>> Mibu's *nembutsu*.

口たゝく夜の往来や花ざかり

kuchi tataku yo no ourai ya hanazakari

> Talking a lot
>> while walking about in the evening –
>>> flowers in full bloom.

巣を守る燕のはらの白さかな

su o mamoru tsubame no hara no shira sakana

> Protecting the nest –
>> the belly of the swallow
>>> like a white fish.

---

[22] Kyogen is a comic interlude between noh plays. However, in this case, it is kyogen nembutsu ("Mibu Dainenbutsu Kyogen") held on the 14th day of the third month for ten days, where there is no dialogue and Buddhistic teachings are illustrated in comic form. Such plays are still performed at Mibu Temple in Kyoto. Formerly, the audience would chant the nembutsu (Hail to Amida Butsu) during the performance.

船よせてさくらぬすむや月夜影

fune yosete sakura nusumu ya tsukiyo kage

> The boat pulled near
>> to steal some blossoms
>>> in the shadows of a moonlit night[23].

二里程は鳶も出て舞ふ汐干哉

ni ri hodo wa tobi mo dete mau shiohi kana

> Five miles[24] about
>> black kites come out and circle –
>>> low tide.

行雁の高キや花につりあはず

yukukari no takaki ya hana ni tsuriawazu

> Departing geese[25] on high –
>> you're out of step
>>> with the blossoms.

---

[23] Taigi has another haiku about the blossom guard in his patrol boat.
[24] Two Japanese *ri*.
[25] In Japan, the geese fly north to their breeding grounds in the spring.

いろいろの名は我言はずさくらかな

iroiro no na wa ware iwazu sakura kana

Of the various names,
   I don't call them
      cherry blossoms[26].

帰る雁きかぬ夜がちに成にけり

kaerukari kikanu yogachi ni nari ni keri

The departing geese –
   determined as usual
      to start off in the evening.

吹はれてまたふる空や春の雪

fuku harete mata furu sora ya haru no yuki

Clear weather is blowing in
   but it's still falling from the sky –
      spring snow.

---

[26] Specifically here in Japanese, *sakura*.

筏士よ足のとまらぬ花ざかり
ikadashi yo ashi no tomaranu hanazakari

> The raftsman!
>> He can't take a break –
>>> flowers are in full bloom.

情なの莟さくらやひなの前
nasakena no tsubomi sakura ya hina no mae

> The budding cherry blossoms
>> look pathetic
>>> beside the Hina Festival dolls[27].

むかひ居てさくらに明す詞かな
mukai ite sakura ni akasu kotoba kana

> Across the way,
>> to put it clearly –
>>> are cherry blossoms!

---

[27] *Hina matsuri*, held the 3rd day of the third lunar month. Also known as Girl's Day. The dolls can be very colourful and elaborate.

散てある椿にみやる木の間かな

chitte aru tsubaki ni miyaru konoma kana

I gaze upon
the camellia blossoms
fallen among the trees.

蝶飛ぶや腹に子ありてねむる猫

chou tobu ya hara ni ko arite nemuru neko

A butterfly in flight –
on the child's stomach,
a sleeping cat.

うばかゝのさくらを覗く彼岸かな

ubakaka no sakura o nozoku higan kana

Higan[28]!
Peeking at
the weeping cherries[29].

---

[28] Buddhist observances held at spring and autumn equinoxes. The autumn observance is often referred to as *aki-higan*, the spring, just *higan*. The sun sets due west at this time.

[29] *Prunus pendula* 'Pleno-rosea'. Also known in Japanese as *ubahigan*.

涅槃会や礼いひありく十五日

nehane ya rei ii ariku juugonichi

> Nirvana Day[30] –
> > repeating the traditional words of gratitude
> > > on the fifteenth.

はる雨や音もいろいろに初夜のかね

haru ame ya ne mo iroiro ni shoya no kane

> Spring rain!
> > The eight o'clock tolling[31]
> > > blends with the various sounds.

ちるなどゝみへぬ若さやはつ桜

chiru nado do mienu wakasa ya hatsu sakura

> They've just come out,
> > can't see many falling –
> > > first cherry blossoms.

---

30 The Buddha's entrance into Nirvana was celebrated on the 15th day of the second lunar month. A statue was held up and a recitation said from the Paranirvana Sutra.

31 Temple bells marked the time of day (2-hour periods), in this case "first night", the hour of the dog at about 8:00 p.m.

陽炎や筏木かはく岸の上
kagerou ya ikada ki kawaku kishi no ue

> Shimmering heat
>> off the dry wooden raft
>>> atop the bank.

すみの江に高き櫓やおぼろ月
suminoe ni takaki yagura ya oborozuki

> High above the tower
>> at Suminoe[32]
>>> the moon shrouded in mist.

春寒し泊瀬の廊下の足のうら
harusamushi hase no rouka no ashi no ura

> Along the corridor of Hasedera Temple[33]
>> the spring cold
>>> on the soles of one's feet.

---

[32] Sumiyoshi, the famous literary locale, near Osaka.
[33] A major Shingon temple in Sakurai, Nara Prefecture. The corridor is likely the 200 metre long covered stairway leading to the temple.

見え初て夕汐みちぬ芦の角
mie hatsute yuushio michinu ashi no tsuno

Their first appearance –
　　reed sprouts
　　　　in the ebbing tide.

かげろふや夜べの網干す川の岸
kagerou ya yobe no ami hosu kawa no kishi

Heat shimmering
　　from the nets left to dry
　　　　on the riverbank last night.

籠舁に山の名を問ふかすみ哉
kagokaki ni yama no na o tou kasumi kana

In the haze,
　　asking the palanquin bearer
　　　　the name of the mountain.

陽炎や板とりて干す池のふね

kagerou ya ita torite hosu ike no fune

> Shimmering heat
> from the planks of the pond boat
> taken out to dry.

はつ午やもの問初る一の橋

hatsuuma ya mono toi hatsuru ichi no hashi

> First Day of the Horse[34]!
> People begin to ask for things
> right from the first bridge[35].

うぐひすや君こぬ宿の経机

uguisu ya kun konu yado no kyouzukue

> Bush warbler!
> Don't come and set up house
> in the sutra-reading desk.

---

[34] The first day of the horse (zodiac) in February. The fox god Inari is worshipped on this day and favours are asked for a good harvest or successful business. The shrine here is the main Inari shrine, in Kyoto, Fushimi Inari Taisho.

[35] Two bridges on the way to the shrine, over the Imakumano River in Kyoto, are named "First Bridge" and "Second Bridge."

踏つけし雪解にけり深山寺

fumitsukeshi yukidoke ni keri miyamadera

> Tramping
>> on the melting snow –
>>> temple deep in the mountains.

初午や狐つくねしあまり土

hatsuuma ya kitsune tsukune shi amari tsuchi

> First Day of the Horse –
>> fox meatball[36] leftovers
>>> scattered on the ground.

濡れて来し雨をふるふや猫の妻

nurete koshi ame o furuu ya neko no tsuma

> She comes in wet with rain
>> and shakes it off –
>>> the cat in heat!

---

[36] I presume this is the name of a dish (e.g. there is Inari sushi) as opposed to actual fox meat. Usually chicken is used and cooked *yakitori* style. See second previous footnote for further information.

34

挑灯で若鮎を売る光かな

chouchin de wakaayu o uru hikari kana

> By the light
> of the paper lantern,
> selling young sweetfish.

霄月や船にもさくら打かたげ

yoizuki ya fune ni mo sakura utsu katage

> Crescent moon[37]!
> Hanging branches of blossoms
> brush the boat.

水吸に鼠出けり瓶の花

mizu suu ni nezumi ide keri bin no hana

> A mouse came out
> and sipped the water –
> flowers in a vase.

---

[37] Specifically the waxing crescent moon, visible only in the evening, from the 2nd to 7th day of the lunar month. It usually refers to the eighth month, but "cherry blossoms" (translated as "blossoms") is the *kigo* (season word) here.

鶴を画く雲井の空や鶏合
tsuru o egaku kumoi no sora ya niwatori ai

    Painting a crane
        high amid the clouds in the sky –
            outside a troop of chickens!

髭につく飯さへみえずねこの妻
hige ni tsuku meshi sae miezu neko no tsuma

    She can't see the food
        stuck on her whiskers –
            the cat in heat!

物音は人にありけりおぼろ月
monooto wa hito ni ari keri oborozuki

    Those sounds,
        they come from that person –
            the moon shrouded in mist!

はる雨や風呂いそがする旅の暮
harusame ya furo isoga suru tabi no kure

> Spring rain
>> I hurry to the bath –
>>> home from my journey.

帰来て灰にもいねず猫の妻
kiraite hai ni mo inezu neko no tsuma

> Ashes to ashes,
>> she won't be going home again –
>>> the cat in heat.

うつくしき男もちたる雉子かな
utsukushiki otoko mochitaru kigisu kana

> Beautiful!
>> The pheasant[38]
>>> that man is carrying.

---

[38]   Green pheasant (*Phasianus versicolor*).

ぬす人の梅やうかゞふ夜の庵

nusubito no ume ya ukagau yoru no io

Evening at the hermitage –
  hearing about
    the plum blossom thief.

白雲や雪解の沢へうつる空

shiragumo ya yukige no sawa e utsuru sora

The white clouds!
  The sky in harmony
    with the melting snow on the marsh.

紅梅や公家町こして日枝山

beniume ya kugemachi koshite hieisan

Red plum blossoms!
  Crossing over Mt. Hiei[39]
    to the Imperial City[40].

---

[39] The famous Mt. Hiei near Kyoto but using different kanji. Basho and Issa both used a similar "spelling."
[40] Kyoto.

閑かさを覗く雨夜の柳かな

shizukasa o nozoku amayo no yanagi kana

> Silence –
>> glancing at the willow
>>> in the evening rain.

駕に居て東風に向ふやふところ手

kako ni ite kochi ni mukau ya futokorode

> Sitting in the palanquin,
>> facing the east wind,
>>> hands inside my kimono[41].

白魚やきよきにつけてなまぐさき

shirauo ya kiyoki ni tsukete namagusaki

> Whitefish[42]!
>> The fishy smell comes along
>>> with its purity.

---

[41] This would be chest level, to keep the hands warm. The same term, *futokoro*, now refers to pockets. This is a winter phrase but "east wind" is spring.

[42] Icefish.

若くさや四角に切し芝の色

wakakusa ya shikaku ni setsu shi shiba no iro

New spring grass,
    mowed to the four corners[43] –
        the colour of the lawn!

若草ややがて田になるやすめ畑

wakakusa ya yagate ta ni naru yasume hata

New spring growth –
    the fallow field
        becomes a rice paddy!

うぐひすや月日覚える親の側

uguisu ya gappi oboeru oya no soba

The bush warbler!
    Next to his parents
        the child memorizes dates.

行春や旅へ出て居る友の数
yukuharu ya tabi e dete iru tomo no kazu

    Spring is passing!
        With a number of friends
            I set out on a journey.

夜歩く春の余波や芝居者
yoru aruku haru no yoha ya shibaimono

    An evening walk,
        the spring waters have calmed –
            the actor.

春ふかし伊勢を戻りし一在所
harufukashi ise o modorishi ichi zaisho

    Spring at its peak,
        I return to Ise,
            the best place to go.

女見る春も名残やわたし守

onna miru haru mo nagori ya watashimori

> He sees the woman
> > and that spring is passing –
> > > the ferryman.

人追ふて蜂もどりけり花の上

hito oute hachi modori keri hana no ue

> He chased the bee
> > but it went back
> > > on top of the flower.

腹立て水呑蜂や手水鉢

haradachite mizunomi hachi ya temizuhachi

> The bee drinking the water
> > is getting angry –
> > > the garden washbasin.

声立て居代る蜂や花の蝶

koetatete i dairu hachi ya hana no chou

> The loud buzz of the bees
> > by the house has been replaced –
> > > butterflies on the flowers!

見初ると日々に蝶みる旅路かな

misomeru to hibi ni chou miru tabiji kana

> The first time seen in days –
> > I gaze at the butterflies
> > > as I journey along.

山吹や葉に花に葉に花に葉に

yamabuki ya ha ni hana ni ha ni hana ni ha ni

> *Yamabuki* yellow rose –
> > leaves, flowers, leaves,
> > > flowers, leaves[44].

---

[44]   This is worth sounding out in the original Japanese.

春の夜や女を怖す作りごと
haru no yoru ya onna o odosu tsukurigoto

> Spring evening –
>> A lie frightens
>>> the woman!

炉ふさぎや老の機嫌の俄事
rofusagi ya oi no kigen no niwakagoto

> Closing up the hearth!
>> A sudden urge
>>> comes upon the old woman.

墨染のうしろすがたや壬生念仏
sumizome no ushiro sugata ya mibunenbutsu

> From the rear
>> the form of the monks[45] –
>>> Mibu Nembutsu[46].

---

[45]   The monks are wearing black robes.
[46]   The kyogen nembutsu ("Mibu Dainenbutsu Kyogen") held on the 14th day
       of the third month for ten days, where there is no dialogue and Buddhistic
       teachings are illustrated in comic form. Such plays are still performed at
       Mibu Temple in Kyoto.

御僧のその手嗅たや御身拭
onsou no sono te kagita ya ominufuku

    The honourable monk
       sniffs his hands
          then wipes the honourable statue[47].

華の色や頭の雪もたとえもの
ka no iro ya atama no yuki mo tatoe mono

    The colour of the blossoms –
       it's just like
          my snowy locks!

陽炎や景清入れし洞の口
kagerou ya kagekiyo ireshi hora no kuchi

    Shimmering heat!
       Kagekiyo[48]
          enters the mouth of the cave.

---

[47] A Buddhist ritual held on the 19th day of the third month where the principal temple image is cleaned with a white cloth. The ceremony at Chionji Temple is especially famous.

[48] Heike general Taira no Kagekiyo. Legend says that the hid in a cave, now in Mine City, Yamaguchi Prefecture, after the Battle of Dan-no-Ura. I envision Taigi entering a cave on a hot day and then Kagekiyo came to mind.

世を宇治の門にも寝るや茶つみ共

yo o uji no kado ni mo neru ya chatsumidomo

> As the world sleeps
>> outside the gates of Uji[49] –
>>> tea pickers!

やぶ入の寐るやひとりの親の側

yabuiri no neru ya hitori no oya no soba

> Sleeping
>> on Servant's Holiday[50]
>>> beside her mother.

ちる花の雪の草鞋や二王門

chiru hana no yuki no waraji ya nioumon

> Snow-like blossoms
>> fall on my straw sandals
>>> by the Nio gate[51].

---

[49]   A famous tea producing area near Kyoto.
[50]   On the 16th day of the first month (right after the New Year period), servants
      were given time off to visit their hometown.
[51]   The gate at an entrance to a temple that houses two fierce *deva* guardians
      known as Nio in Japan.

蛙居て啼やうき藻の上と下

kaeru ite naku ya uki mo no uetoshita

    Frogs croaking!
      Above and below
         the floating duckweed.

出代や厩は馬にいとまごひ

degawari ya umaya wa uma ni itomagoi

    Change of servants day[52] –
      he says goodbye
         to the horse in the stable.

養父入の兒けばけばし草の宿

youfu iri no bau kebakebashi kusa no yado

    The adoptive father,
      gaudily dressed,
         enters the lowly inn.

---

[52] Servants were contracted for six months or a year and replaced after that period. In Taigi's time it was done on the 5th day of the third month (and the ninth month).

出代やきのふからいふいとまごひ

degawari ya kinou kara iu itomagohi

Change of servants day –
    since yesterday
        she's been saying her goodbyes.

京中の未見ぬ寺や遅桜

miyako naka no mi minu tera ya osozakura

In Kyoto,
    the temples can't be seen –
        late blooming cherry blossoms!

したゝかなさくらかたげて夜道かな

shitatakana sakura katagete yomichi kana

A myriad cherry blossoms
    hang over the road
        at night!

あるじする乳母よ御針よ庭の花
aruji suru uba yo o hari yo niwa no hana

    The mistress
        is a wet nurse, a seamstress …
            a blossom in the garden.

身をやつし御庭みる日や遅桜
mi o yatsushi oniwa miru hi ya osozakura

    In the sunshine I'm absorbed
        in gazing at my honourable garden –
            late cherry blossoms!

塵はみなさくら也けり寺の暮
chiri wa mina sakura nari keri tera no kure

    Littering the ground –
        it's all fallen blossoms!
            The temple at dusk.

田螺みへて風腥し水のうへ
tanishi miete kaze namagusashi mizu no ue

    Gazing at the river snail[53] –
       the wind over the water
          smelling of fish.

朝風呂はけふの桜の機嫌哉
asaburo wa kyou no sakura no kigen kana

    The morning bath –
       today feels like
          cherry blossom season!

ふりむけば灯とぼす関や夕霞
furimukeba hi tobosu seki ya yuugasumi

    If you look back you'll see
       the barrier lights being lit
          through the twilight mist.

---

[53] *Viviparidae.*

崖路行寺の背や松の藤

gakemichi yuku ji no sei ya matsu no fuji

    From the cliffside road
        to the temple on the ridge –
            the pines look like wisteria!

大船の岩におそる〻霞かな

oobune no iwa ni osoreru kasumi kana

    In the mist,
        the rocks by the big boat
            are frightening.

山独活に木賃の飯の忘られぬ

yama udo ni kichin no meshi no wasurarenu

    I'll never forget
        the meal of spikenard[54]
            at the humble inn[55] in the mountains.

---

[54]   *Aralia cordata*. The stems are cooked and served in miso soup.

[55]   A cheap inn where you bring your own food and pay for the firewood and water etc. used for cooking.

つみ草や背に負ふ子も手まさぐり

tsumikusa ya se ni ou ko mo temasaguri

    The dayflower!
        The child carried on her back
            twiddles it in his fingers.

あなかまと鳥の巣みせぬ菴主哉

anakama to tori no su misenu anshu kana

    "Be quiet!"
        The master of hermitage is showing
            where the bird's nest is.

落て啼く子に声かはす雀かな

ochite naku ko ni koe kawasu suzume kana

    The sparrow
        answers the cry
            of the fallen fledgling.

紫の塵やつもりて問屋もの
murasaki no chiri ya tsumorite tonya mono

    Bracken buds!
       They pile up
          at the wholesaler's.

来るとはや往来数ある燕かな
kuru to haya yukiki kazu aru tsubame kana

    Already they've arrived!
       Many swallows can be seen
          coming and going.

摘草やよそにも見ゆる母娘
tsumikusa ya yoso ni mo miyuru oyako

    Gathering spring greens!
       Elsewhere too
          mothers and daughters can be seen.

人おとにこけ込亀や春の水

hito oto ni kokekomu kame ya haru no mizu

> At the sound of someone coming
>> the turtle plunged into the water –
>>> spring run-off.

奉る花に手ならぬわらびかな

tatematsuru hana ni te naranu warabi kana

> Reverently offering flowers –
>> don't include bracken[56]
>>> in the bouquet.

行舟に岸根をうつや春の水

yuku fune ni kishine o utsu ya haru no mizu

> The passing boat,
>> strikes the submerged bank –
>>> spring run-off.

---

[56] Bracken is a coarse fern not as "delicate" as the flowers.

穂は枯て接木の台の芽立けり

ho wa karete tsugiki no dai no medachi keri

    The tips of the grafted sprouts
        on the stand
            are withered.

鶯の目には籠なき高音かな

uguisu no me ni wa kago naki takane kana

    The eyes of the bush warbler
        with its high-pitched singing
            in the cage.

堀川や家の下行春の水

horikawa ya uchi no shimo yuku haru no mizu

    By canal
        travelling downstream back home –
            spring run-off.

うぐひすや葉の動く水の笹がくれ

uguisu ya ha no ugoku mi no sasa ga kure

> The bush warbler!
>> The leaves are moving where it hides
>>> in the bamboo[57] by the water.

うぐひすの声せで来けり苔の上

uguisu no koe sede ki keri koke no ue

> The bush warbler
>> came across the moss
>>> silently.

出替りの畳へおとすなみだかな

degawari no tatami e otosu namida kana

> Change of servants day[58] –
>> her tears
>>> fall on the *tatami* mat.

---

[57] *Sasa japonica*.

[58] Servants were contracted for six months or a year and replaced after that period. In Taigi's time it was done on the 5th day of the third month (and the ninth month).

ふらこゝの会釈こぼるゝや高みより
furakoko no eshaku koboreru ya takami yori

From the swing she nods,
all the way up –
so high!

付まとふ内義の沙汰や花ざかり
tsukimatou naigi no sata ya hanazakari

Following me about
a secret is being whispered –
the blossoms are in full bloom!

花守のあづかり船や岸の月
hanamori no azukari fune ya kishi no tsuki

The patrol boat
of the blossom guard –
moonlight on the shore.

介子推お七がやうになられけむ

kaishisui oshichi ga yau ni narare kemu

Jie Zhitui[59] and Yaoya Oshichi[60]
   are quite alike –
      they both went up in smoke[61].

不自由なる手で候よ花のもと

fujiyuunaru te de sourou yo hana no moto

My hands
   are sun-burned.
      Under the shade of the blossoms!

---

[59]   A loyal retainer of Duke Wen of Jin (7th cent. BCE) who in later life became a mountain recluse living with his mother. When he would not return to court the Duke had a fire set on the mountain to flush him out but Jie and his mother died in the flames. Veneration of his spirit eventually led to the Cold Food and Qingming Festivals, both spring events.

[60]   (1667–1683). The daughter of a greengrocer, she fled a major fire in 1682 and took refuge in a monastery. There she fell in love with a pageboy. The next year she tried to set a fire in town so she could meet him again but was caught and burned at the stake on March 29.

[61]   Besides being real people, remember these are also literary characters, especially Yaoya, who was portrayed in kabuki plays as well as Saikaku's *Five Women Who Loved Love*.

鞦韆や隣みこさぬ御身躰
shuusen ya tonari mukosanu onkarada

    The swing!
       I didn't foresee
          my neighbour's honourable body!

菜の花やよし野下来る向ふ山
nanohana ya yoshino shita kuru mukau yama

    Rape blossoms!
       Coming down from Yoshino[62],
          approaching the mountains.

下萌や土の裂目の物の色
shimomoe ya tsuchi no sakeme no mono no iro

    Spring sprouts!
       Colours tear up
          from the soil.

---

[62]   A famous old area near Nara.

東風吹や道行人の面にも

kochi fuku ya michi koujin no omote ni mo

> An east wind is blowing!
>> The look on the people's faces
>>> travelling along the road.

親に逢に行出代や老の坂

oya ni ai ni yuku degawari ya oi no saka

> Going to meet her parents
>> on change of servants day[63] –
>>> the hardships of old age[64].

やぶ入や琴かき鳴す親の前

yabuiri ya koto kakinasu oya no mae

> Servant's Holiday![65]
>> Playing the *koto*
>>> before her parents.

---

[63] Servants were contracted for six months or a year and replaced after that period. In Taigi's time it was done on the 5th day of the third month (and the ninth month).

[64] Literally the "slope or hill of old age." An idiom that compares growing old with climbing a hill.

[65] On the 16th day of the first month (right after the New Year period), servants were given time off to visit their hometown.

出替や朝飯すはる胸ふくれ

degawari ya asameshi suwaru mune fukure

Change of servant's day!
    Sitting down to breakfast,
        his chest swollen with emotion.

川の香のほのかに東風の渡りけり

kawa no ka no honoka ni kochi no watari keri

The faint fragrance of the river
    comes drifting across
        in the east wind.

雉子追ふて呵られて出る畠哉

kiji oute shikararete deru hatake kana

Scolding and chasing
    a pheasant
        out of the garden.

御影供やひとの問よる守敏塚

mieiku ya hito no toi yoru shubin tsuka

Kukai's Memorial day[66] –
   someone asks for
      Shubin's[67] burial mound!

蚕飼ふ女やふるき身だしなみ

kaikokau onna ya furuki midashinami

The silkworm farmer –
   her old-time
      conservative appearance!

葉隠れの機嫌伺ふ桑子哉

hagakure no kigen ukagau kuwako kana

I ask
   why silkworms
      like to hide in the leaves.

---

[66]   Kukai or Kobo Daishi (774–835), the founder of the Shingon Sect of
       Buddhism and a major figure in Japanese religion and culture.
[67]   Dates unknown. A rival monk to Kukai who unsuccessfully tried to kill him.

ゆたゆたと畝へだて来る雉子かな
yutayuta to une e date kuru kijishi kana

    Calm and relaxed
      it comes up the ridge –
        the pheasant!

長閑さや早き月日を忘れたる
nodokasa ya hayaki tsukihi o wasuretaru

    Tranquillity –
      forgetting how the days and months
        fly by!

遅き日を見るや眼鏡を懸ながら
osoki hi o miru ya megane o kakenagara

    When I see the day
      is getting late,
        I put on my glasses!

春風にてらすや騎射の綾藺笠

harukaze ni terasu ya kisha no ayaikasa

> Shining in the spring breeze –
> the conical hats
> of the equestrian archers!

燕来てなき人問ん此彼岸

tsubame kite naki hito tou n kono higan

> The swallows arrive
> for this *higan*[68]
> without people even asking.

矢橋乗る嫁よむすめよ春の風

yabase noru yome yo musume yo haru no kaze

> My daughter, the bride,
> arrives at Yabase[69]
> in the breezes of spring.

---

[68] Buddhist observances held at spring and autumn equinoxes. The autumn observance is often referred to as *aki-higan*, the spring, just *higan*. The sun sets due west at this time.

[69] Yabase, a former port town on Lake Biwa. I have assumed the daughter to be Taigi's.

草をはむ胸安からじ猫の恋

kusa o hamu mune yasukaraji neko no koi

> The agitated
>   cat in heat
>   is eating the grass.

諫めつゝ繋ぎ居にけり猫の恋

isametsutsu tsunagi kyo ni keri neko no koi

> Even though admonished
>   it loiters in the house for now –
>   cat in heat.

声真似る小者おかしや猫の恋

koe maneru komono okashi ya neko no koi

> Mimicking the voice
>   of a strange youth –
>   the cat in heat.

遅き日を膝へ待とる番所かな

osoki hi o hiza e matsu toru bansho kana

>   It's getting late –
>   the guardsman is waiting
>   to sit and have his meal.

春の日や午時も門掃く人心

haru no hi ya goji mo kado haku hitogokoro

>   Spring sunshine –
>   it's human nature
>   to sweep the entrance midday.

おもひ寐の耳に動くや猫の恋

omoi ne no mimi ni ugoku ya neko no koi

>   I believe its ears twitched
>   as it was sleeping –
>   the cat in heat!

耕すやむかし右京の土の艶

tagayasu ya mukashi ukyou no tsuchi no en

> Tilling the land –
>> ah! the beauty of the soil
>>> of ancient Ukyo![70]

はる雨や芝居みる日も旅姿

harusame ya shibai miru hi mo tabisugata

> Spring rain!
>> A day to go see a play
>>> in my travelling outfit.

野をやくや荒くれ武士の畑草の火

no o yaku ya arakure bushi no tabako no hi

> The field's burning!
>> It was a gruff samurai
>>> lighting his tobacco.

---

[70] The old western section of Kyoto.

春雨や昼間経よむおもひもの

harusame ya hiruma kyou yomu omohimono

> Spring rain!
> > During the day
> > > the concubine[71] reads the sutras.

畑うつやいづくはあれど京の土

hata utsu ya izuku wa aredo kyou no tsuchi

> Tilling the soil!
> > Where, anyway,
> > > is there land in Kyoto?

江をわたる漁村の犬や芦の角

e o wataru gyoson no inu ya ashi no tsuno

> Crossing the bay, I see
> > the dogs of the fishing village –
> > > sprouting reeds.

---

[71] It could be the concubine of Taigi but I have left it in a general sense here and elsewhere.

皮ひてし穢多が入江や芦の角

kawa hite shi eta ga irie ya ashi no tsuno

    Drying the hides by the cove,
      the *eta*[72] –
        sprouting reeds.

実の為に枝たはめじな梨の花

mi no tame ni eda tawamejina nashi no hana

    The bending branches
      are a real benefit –
        pear blossoms!

月更て朧の底の野風哉

tsuki sarate oboro no soko no nokaze kana

    The wind blown fields
      lie beneath
        the sinking hazy moon.

---

[72] An Edo low-caste group whose work usually involved handling human bodies or animal carcasses.

島原へ愛宕もどりやおぼろ月

shimabara e atago modori ya oborozuki

> Returning from Atago[73]
> to Shimabara[74] –
> the misty moon!

連翹や黄母衣の衆の屋敷町

rengyou ya kiboro no shuu no yashikimachi

> Weeping forsythia!
> A mass of warriors in yellow cloaks[75]
> in the samurai district.

欺て行キぬけ寺やおぼろ月

azamuite yukinuke tera ya oborozuki

> It's deceiving –
> languidly passing over the temple,
> the hazy moon.

---

[73] Atago Shrine on Mt. Atago.

[74] The red-light district of Kyoto where Taigi lived.

[75] *Hori* were cloaks that samurai horsemen wore on their backs to help protect against arrows and especially connected with Hideyoshi. *Kibori* were such cloaks in a yellow colour. I can only assume that in Edo times they were worn at some festivity. Weeping forsythia, of course, are yellow.

海の鳴南やおぼろおぼろ月

umi no nari minami ya oboro oborozuki

> The rumbling of the sea
>   to the south –
>   a hazy, hazy moon.

川下に網うつ音やおぼろ月

kawashimo ni ami utsu oto ya oborozuki

> Downstream, the sound of nets
>   striking the water –
>   hazy moon.

こゝろゆく極彩色や涅槃像

kokoro yuku gokusaishoku ya nehanzou

> The rich colours
>   go straight to the heart –
>   Buddha's Paranirvana statue[76].

---

[76] The depiction of Buddha lying on his side in his final moments before entering Nirvana.

起々に蒟蒻もらふ彼岸かな

oki oki ni konnyaku morau higan kana

> Waking up
>> I get *konnyaku* jelly[77] –
>>> it's *higan!*[78]

引寄て折手をぬける柳かな

hikiyosete orite o nukeru yanagi kana

> Pulling it up
>> with my hands,
>>> the willow's uprooted.

ねはむ会に来てもめでたし嵯峨の釈迦

nehane ni kite mo medetashi saga no shaka

> Auspiciously coming
>> on Nirvana Day[79],
>>> the Buddha of Saga[80].

---

[77] A still popular Japanese food made from konjac rhizomes.
[78] Buddhist observances held at spring and autumn equinoxes
[79] The Buddha's entrance into Nirvana was celebrated on the 15th day of the second lunar month. A statue was held up and a recitation said from the Paranirvana Sutra.
[80] Formerly at the boundary of Kyoto near Arashiyama.

里の子や髪に結なす春の草

sato no ko ya kami ni yui nasu haru no kusa

    The village children!
        Their hair done up
            with spring grasses.

丸盆に八幡みやげの弓矢かな

marubon ni hachimon miyage no yumiya kana

    A bow and arrow!
        A Hachimon[81] gift
            on the circular tray.

色色に谷のこたへる雪解かな

iroiro ni tani no kotaeru yukido kana

    The valley responds
        with a variety of colours
            to the melting snow.

---

[81] The Japanese god of archery and war. He was also known as *yumiyahachimon* or "bow & arrow Hachimon," so this may be just wordplay.

花店に二寸短し富貴の薹
hanadana ni futaki mijikashi tomi no tou

> At the flower shop
>   expensive butterbur stalks
>   two and a half inches short!

情なふ蛤乾く余寒かな
nasakenau hamaguri kawaku yokan kana

> The clams
>   are pathetic
>   as winter lingers on!

元船の水汲うらや蕗の薹
motobune no mizukumi ura ya fukinotou

> The main boat[82] is drawing water
>   near the shore –
>   butterbur sprouts!

---

[82] A large boat that has a smaller boat attached to it.

紅梅や大きな弥陀に光さす
koubai ya ookina mita ni hikari sasu

    Red plum blossoms!
      Lit up by the light shining
         on the large Amida statue.

春もやゝ遠目に白しむめの花
haru mo yaya toume ni shiroshi mume no hana

    Plum blossoms
      seen white in the distance
         bring a little spring.

紅梅の散るやわらべの帋つゝみ
koubai no chiru ya warabe no kami tsutsumi

    Red plum blossoms fall!
      Wrapping paper
         for the children.

な折そと折てくれけり園の梅

na oriso to orite kure keri sono no ume

    "Don't break it off!"
       Then he broke it off for me –
          plum blossoms in the garden.

糊おける絹に東風行門辺哉

nori okeru kinu ni kochi yuki mon he kana

    The eastern breeze
       blows the starched silk
          hanging near the gate.

春風や薙刀持の目八分

harukaze ya naginata motsu no mehachibun

    The spring breeze!
       Holding the long sword[83]
          below eye level.

---

[83]   A *naginata*, a weapon having a blade affixed to a long wooden pole.

虚無僧のあやしく立り塀の梅

komusou no ayashiku tatari hei no ume

There was a suspicious Zen monk[84]
　　standing there by the fence
　　　　where the plum blossoms are.

梅活て月とも侘んともし影

ume ikete tsuki to mo wabin tomoshikage

The plum blossom arrangement –
　　as quiet a beauty in lantern light
　　　　as moonlight.

家遠き大竹はらや残る雪

ie tooki ootake hara ya nokoru yuki

Far from home,
　　snow lingering
　　　　in the fields of Otake[85].

---

[84]　Specifically, a begging Zen priest of the Fuke sect who wore "straw basket" headgear and played the *shakuhachi,* a vertical bamboo flute). Many were former *ronin* (masterless samurai) during the Edo period.

[85]　There is an Otake in Hiroshima Prefecture. Blyth translates *ootake* literally as "great bamboos."

春駒やよい子育し小屋の者
harukoma ya yoi ko sodate shi koya no mono

   Horses in spring!
     Fine ponies
       raised in the stables.

物深き夜の櫻や寺の門
mono fukaki yoru no sakura ya tera no mon

     Set back
       from the temple gate –
         cherry blossoms in the evening.

春の夜や昼雉子うちし気の弱り
haru no yo ya hiru kiji uchishi ki no yowari

     A spring evening –
       striking that pheasant today,
    now I feel down.

よく答う若侍や青すだれ

yoku kotau wakazamurai ya ao sudare

　　The young samurai
　　　　answers properly –
　　　　　　the verdant bamboo blind.

落かゝる夕べの鐘やいかのぼり

ochikakaru yuube no kane ya ikanobori

　　The bells of evening
　　　　are about to sound –
　　　　　　kites!

早乙女の下りたつあのたこの田哉

saotome no oritatsu ano tako no ta kana

　　That kite in the field
　　　　moving up and down
　　　　　　is a young woman planting rice.

逢ひ見しは女の賊や朧月
aimishi wa onna no suri ya oborozuki

    Face to face
        with the woman thief –
            the moon shrouded in mist.

藤いけてしおれしまゝや旅の宿
fuji ikete shioreshi mama ya tabi no yado

    At the travel inn
        the wisteria arrangement
            has withered.

長き日や目のつかれたろ海の上
nagaki hi ya me no tsukaretaru umi no ue

    A long day!
        My eyes are tired
            gazing out to sea.

屋根に寝る主なし猫や春の雨

yaru ni neru nushi nashi neko ya haru no ame

An alley cat
   is sleeping on the roof
      in the spring rain.

Summer

草の戸や畳かへたる夏祓

kusa no to ya tatami ka hetaru natsubarae

In my humble hut
    changing the *tatami* mats –
        summer exorcism[86]!

むし干やむかしの旅のはさみ箱

mushiboshi ya mukashi no tabi no hasamibako

Summer airing[87] –
    the scissors box
        from that trip of long ago.

むし干や抜身をさます松の風

mushiboshi ya nukimi o samasu matsu no kaze

Summer airing!
    The wind from the pines
        cools my sword blade.

---

[86] *Natusharae,* a communal Shinto exorcism held on the last day of the sixth
      lunar month. One's body was washed and purified.
[87] A day to remove moisture from all one's belongings after the rainy season.
      The key thing was letting a dry breeze blow through the house to which
      items would be taken out and exposed.

酒蔵に蝿の声きく暑かな

sakagura ni hae no koe kiku atsusa kana

> I listen the sound
>   of the flies in the sake brewery –
>   the heat!

老たりといふや祭の重鎧

oitari to iu ya matsuri no omoyoroi

> Tell the old folk!
>   It's the Festival of
>   Heavy Armour!

酔ふして一村起ぬ祭かな

yoi fushite isson okinu matsuri kana

> Going to bed dead drunk
>   the entire village will not wake up –
>   festival time!

虫ぼしのすゞしさかたれ角櫓
mushiboshi no suzushisa ka tare sumiyagura

The coolness of summer airing day —
  things hanging to dry
    from the corner turret.

屋根茸は屋根で涼の噂かな
yanefuki wa yane de suzushi no uwasa kana

They're thatching the roof —
  I hear
    it's cool up there!

片道はかはきて白し夏の月
katamichi wa kawakite shiroshi natsu no tsuki

Out on a journey,
  I'm so thirsty —
    white summer moon.

まし水にあやうき橋を涼かな
mashi mizu ni ayauki hashi o suzumi kana

> Ah! The coolness
>   on the floating bridge
>   over the clear waters.

関守の背戸口にたつ涼み哉
sekimori no setoguchi ni tatsu suzumi kana

> The checkpoint[88] guard
>   standing by the exit gate
>   cooling off!

汗とりや弓に肩ぬぐ袖のうち
asetori ya yumi ni katanugu sode no uchi

> In my undergarments –
>   after archery, I went in
>   and stripped off my outer clothes.

---

[88]   Likely on the old Tokaido road from Kyoto to Edo.

早鮓に平相国の鱸かな

hayazushi ni heishoukoku no suzuki kana

> The sea bass
>   of Taira no Kiyomori[89]
>   is in the *haya* sushi[90].

はや鮓の蓋とる迄の唱和かな

hayazushi no futa toru made no shouwa kana

> We chanted rounds
>   until we lifted
>   the weight off the *haya* sushi.

かゝる日や今年も一度心太

kakaru hi ya kotoshi mo ichido tokoroten

> The sun's high in the sky!
>   Once again this year –
>   gelidium jelly[91].

---

[89] In the *Tales of Heike,* a large sea bass jumps into Kiyomori's boat and a
      priest tells him it is an auspicious sign and to eat it write away. Taira no
      Kiyomori (1118–1181) established the first samurai government.
[90] A type of sushi with pickled fish and rice, lightly pressed overnight.
[91] Made of agar from red algae. Used in preparing various delicacies.

帷子や蝿のつといる袖のうち
katabira ya hae no tsuto iru sode no uchi

    Summer kimono –
        suddenly, a fly
            flew up the sleeve!

夕立や扇にうけし下り蜘
yuudachi ya ougi ni ukeshi kudari kumo

    Evening shower –
        floating down to the fan,
            a spider!

鵜ぶねみる岸や闇路をたどりたどり
ubune miru kishi ya yamiji o tadoritadori

    I see the cormorant fishing boats
        offshore –
            I'm lost on this dark road.

木枕に耳のさはりて暑き也

komakura ni mimi no sawarite atsuki nari

My ear
    on the wooden pillow –
        it feels hot!

松明に雨乞行やよるの嶺

taimatsu ni amagoigyou ya yoru no mine

We go praying for rain
    by torchlight –
        the mountain peaks at night.

かたびらの無理な節句や傘の下

katabira no murina sekku ya kasa no shita

My summer kimono
    for the festival is inappropriate –
        under the umbrella.

五月雨や川うちわたす蓑の裾
samidare ya kawa uchiwatasu mino no suso

    Fifth Month rain –
        crossing the river,
            bottom of my straw raincoat wet.

松陰に旅人帯とく暑かな
matsukage ni tabito obi toku atsusa kana

    In the shade of a pine,
        the traveller undoes his sash –
            the heat!

漣にうしろ吹るゝ田植かな
sazanami ni ushiro fukareru taue kana

    The wind blows ripples
        on the water
            behind the rice planters.

子子やなまなか澄るくされ水
boufura ya namanaka sumiru kusare mizu

　　Mosquito larvae –
　　　half cleared out
　　　　of the putrid pool.

草の戸や竹植る日を覚書
kusa no to ya takeueru hi o oboegaki

　　My humble hut –
　　　a note to remember
　　　　bamboo planting day.

さみだれや夜明見はづす旅の宿
samidare ya yoake mihazusu tabi no yado

　　Early summer rain –
　　　I missed seeing daybreak
　　　　at the traveller's inn.

掃流す橋の埃や夏の月
souryuusu hashi no hokori ya natsu no tsuki

    Sweeping
        the dust from the bridge –
            summer moon.

寺からも婆を出されし田植哉
tera kara mo baba o dasareshi taue kana

    Again, the old woman
        exits the temple –
            rice planting season!

とりにがす隣の声や行ほたる
tori ni gasu tonari no koe ya yuku hotaru

    The neighbour's voice
        applauding the catch –
            the fireflies fly off.

わびしげや麦の穂なみにかくれ妻
wabishige ya mugi no minorunami ni kakure tsuma

 It's pitiful!
  The wife hiding
   amid the ears of wheat.

思案して旅の袷にうつりけり
shian shite tabi no awase ni utsuri keri

 On second thought
  I changed into a summer kimono
   for the journey.

ぼうふりや蓮の浮葉の露の上
boufuri ya hasu no ukiha no tsuyu no ue

 Mosquito larvae –
  dew on the floating leaves
   of the lotus.

塩魚も庭の雫やさつきあめ

shiozakana mo niwa no shizuku ya satsuki ame

> Salted fish too,
>   dripping in the garden –
>   early summer rain.

影高き松にのぞむや蝸牛

kage takaki matsu ni nozomu ya katatsumuri

> In the shade of a tall pine,
>   gazing
>   at a snail.

岩角や火縄すり消す苔の花

iwakado ya hinawa suri kesu koke no hana

> The edge of a rock!
>   I extinguish the fuse[92] –
>   flowering moss[93].

---

[92] Used to light tobacco as well as arquebusiers.
[93] Cedar or hair moss. Filaments shoot up when sporing.

ほとゝぎすきくや汗とる夜着の中

hototogisu kiku ya ase toru yogi no naka

> I hear the lesser cuckoo!
> Sweating, I take off
> my quilted nightwear.

旅立を人もうらやむ袷かな

tabidachi o hito mo urayamu awase kana

> I am envious
> of people off on a journey
> in their summer kimonos.

笋やほりつゝ行けばぬいた道

takenoko ya horitsutsu ikeba nuita michi

> Bamboo shoots!
> I hope, when I go,
> to dig some up by the road.

みじかよや旅寐のまくら投わたし
mijikayo ya tabine no makura tou watashi

    Short summer nights –
        putting down my pillow
            for a night's rest on my journey.

手から手へわたしわづらふ蛍かな
te kara te e watashi wazurau hotaru kana

    Flittering from hand to hand,
        it's annoying –
            the firefly!

今朝みれば夜の歩みやかたつむり
kesa mireba yoru no ayumi ya katatsumuri

    This morning
        when I looked where I walked last night –
            a snail!

さみだれや夜半に貝吹まさり水

samidare ya yowa ni kai fuki masari mizu

Early summer rain –
    in the dead of night, a shellfish spits
        a splendid stream of water.

八重雲に朝日のにほふ五月哉

yaegumo ni asahi no niou satsuki kana

The morning sun amid the layered clouds
    is beautiful –
        the fifth month.

若竹や数もなき葉の露の数

wakatake ya kazu mo naki ha no tsuyu no kazu

The new bamboo –
    so much dew
        on so many leaves!

みじか夜や雲引残す富士のみね
mijikayo ya kumo hikinokusu fuji no mine

    The short summer night –
        just a few clouds left
            on Fuji's summit.

蚊の声は打も消さぬよ雨の音
ka no koe wa uchi mo kesanu yo ame no oto

    The buzz of mosquitoes.
        Swat! – can't get ric of them.
            The sound of rain.

一日は物あたらしき五月雨
tsuitachi wa mono atarashiki satsukiame

    First day of the month,
        something new –
            Fifth Month rain.

雨の日は行かれぬ橋やかきつばた
ame no hi wa ikarenu hashi ya kakitsubata

A rainy day –
    I can't go to the bridge
        to view the rabbit-ear iris.

白雨はあなたの空よ鷺の行
shirasame wa anata no sora yo sagi no yuku

A sudden shower –
    in the distant sky,
        herons fly.

たけの子や己が葉分に衝のぼる
takenoko ya onore ga hawake ni shou noboru

Climbing up the road
    I push apart leaves –
        bamboo shoots!

笋やおもひもかけず宇津の山
takenoko ya omoi mo kakezu utsunoyama

Bamboo shoots.
I don't even think
of Mt. Utsu[94].

うつす手に光る蛍や指のまた
utsusu te ni hikaru hotaru ya yubi no mata

Fireflies
light up my hand –
my fingers too!

みじかよや来ると寝に行うき勤
mijikayo ya kuru to ne ni yuku ukitsutome

The short summer night –
sleep arrives
when I'm busy working!

---

[94] Utsunoyama, on the old Tokkaido road at Okabe, near Shizuoka.

蝙蝠や千木みえわかる闇の空

koumori ya chigi mie wakaru yami no sora

> Bats!
>> They can just be seen in the dark sky
>>> by the shrine gables[95].

蛍火や岸にしづまる夜の水

hotarubi ya kishi ni shi zumaru yoru no mizu

> The light of fireflies
>> as it grows quiet by the shore –
>>> the river at night.

麦を打ほこりの先に聟舅

mugi o uchi hokori no saki ni muko shuuto

> Father and son-in-law[96] –
>> afterwards proud of having
>>> threshed the barley.

---

[95] The V-formation at the top of shrines where crossbeams intersect.
[96] Meaning father-in-law and son-in-law.

寐た顔へ蚊帳吹あてるはし居哉

neta kao e kaya fuku ateru hashi i kana

> The mosquito net's edge
>   is blown and touches
>   my face in bed.

みじか夜やむりに寐ならふ老心

mijikayo ya muri ni nenarau oigokoro

> Short summer nights –
>   I'm used to sleeping at any time.
>   Feeling old.

泥の干る池あたらしやた若

doro no hiru ike atarashi ya kakitsubata

> They've just bloomed,
>   in the drying up muddy pond –
>   rabbit-ear iris!

雨に倦く人もこそあれかきつばた

ame ni aku hito mo koso are kakitsubata

Even for those tired of the rain
there's still
the rabbit-ear iris.

あら浪に蝿とまりけり船の腹

aranami ni hae tomari keri fune no hara

The fly that alighted
on the billowing waves
goes under the ship's hull.

用意せし袷出す日や昼旅籠

youi seshi awase desu hi ya hiru hatago

Preparing to go out for the day
in my summer kimono –
my lunch basket.

ほり上てあやめ葺けり茸の庵

hori agete ayame fuki keri kusa no io

    Climbing the moat –
       irises hung
          from the thatched huts[97].

川風に水打ながす晒かな

kawakaze ni mizuuchi nagasu sarashi kana

    A breeze off the river –
       I sprinkle water
          over the bleached cotton.

葉ざくらのひと木淋しや堂の前

hazakura no hito ki sabishi ya dou no mae

    Leaves sprout
       on a solitary cherry tree
          in front of the shrine.

---

[97]Boy's Festival, on the 5th day of the fifth lunar month, derived from an iris festival in China and iris leaves or blooms are hung from the eaves.

年よれば疲もをかし更衣

toshi yoreba wakare mo o kashi koromogae

Because of my age
    my legs again are tired –
        Change of Clothes Day[98].

あまた蚊の血にふくれ居る座禅哉

amata ka no chi ni fukure iru zazen kana

Seated in meditation[99] –
    many mosquitoes about
        swollen with blood.

蝿を打おとや隣もきのふけふ

hae o utsu oto ya tonari mo kinou kyou

The sound of swatting flies
    from my neighbour's –
        yesterday and today too!

---

[98] On the 1st day of the fourth lunar month one changed to summer clothes.
[99] *Zazen*: Zen meditation.

麦秋や埃にかすむ昼の鐘
bakushuu ya hokori ni kasumu hiru no kane

    Harvesting the wheat!
       As the air blurs with dust
          the noon bell tolls.

など我は寝ざめぬ老ぞ時鳥
nado ware wa nezamenu o zo hototogisu

    For old folk like me
       it's hard to wake up –
          the lesser cuckoo!

年よらぬ顔ならべたやはつ鰹
toshi yoranu kao narabeta ya hatsu katsuo

    The year is still young,
       faces lined up –
          the first bonito!

ほとゝぎす江戸のむかしを夢の内

hototogisu edo no mukashi o yume no uchi

> The lesser cuckoo –
> > in a dream of Edo[100]
> > > of long ago.

かきつばたやがて田へとる池の水

kakitsubata yagate ta e toru ike no mizu

> The pond
> > has rabbit-ear iris –
> > > soon we'll harvest the rice.

卯の花はまはりこくらの垣根かな

unohana wa mawarikokura no kakine kana

> The rabbit-flower plant[101] –
> > it's spreading
> > > all around the fence!

ほとゝぎす今見し人へ文使ひ

hototogisu ima mishi hito e bunzukai

> The messenger going there,
>> just now,
>>> saw a lesser cuckoo.

立むかふ広間代りや更衣

tachimukau hiroma kawari ya koromogae

> In the hall
>> standing before and replacing them –
>>> Change of Clothes Day[102].

末摘のあちら向ひてもおどり哉

suetsumu no achira muite mo odori kana

> There's a dance
>> over there
>>> across from the safflowers.

---

[102] On the 1st day of the fourth lunar month one changed to summer clothes.

橋落て人岸にあり夏の月
hashi ochite hito kishi ni ari natsu no tsuki

    The bridge collapsed
        leaving people on the banks –
            summer moon.

白雨やこと鎮めたる使者の馬
shirasame ya koto shizumetaru shisha no uma

    A sudden shower –
        calming down
            the messenger's horse.

夕皃やそこら暮るに白き花
yuugao ya sokora kureru ni shiroki hana

    Moonflowers!
        All about at dusk
            white blossoms.

白雨や戸ざしにもどる艸の庵

shirasame ya tozashi ni modoru kusa no io

A sudden shower![103]
    I return to close the door
        of my thatched hut.

かたびらのそこら縮て昼寐かな

katabira no sokora chijirete hirune kana

My light kimono
    is wrinkled everywhere –
        an afternoon nap!

白雨や膳最中の大書院

shirasame ya zen saichuu no oojoin

A sudden shower!
    Sitting at my dining table
        in the guest room.

---

[103] Blyth, History of Haiku, v2, p. 292, has a variant with *yuudachi*, summer (or evening) shower.

あしらひて巻葉添けり瓶の蓮

ashiraite makiba sou keri bin no hasu

> I arranged the unfurled leaves
>> to my satisfaction –
>>> lotus in a jar.

沢瀉や花の数そふ魚の泡

omodaka ya hana no kazu sou sakana no awa

> Threeleaf arrowhead –
>> the many flower buds look like
>>> fish bubbles[104].

蓮の香や深くも籠る葉の茂

hasu no ka ya fukaku mo komoru ha no shigeru

> The fragrance of the lotus!
>> Hidden away
>>> in their dense foliage.

---

[104] Besides growing in wetlands, the flower buds resemble bubbles from a fish. The Japanese just uses the word "flowers."

空をみてすゞみとる夜や宿直の間
sora o mite suzumi toru yo ya tonoi no ma

> I caught him cooling off,
> > gazing at the evening sky,
> > > during night watch.

来し跡のつくが浅まし蝸牛
koshi ato no tsuku ga asamashi katatsumuri

> Pushing along
> > and leaving a trail –
> > > the lowly snail!

釣瓶から水呑ひとや道の端
tsurube kara mizunomi hito ya michi no hashi

> Someone's drinking water
> > from the well bucket
> > > by the side of the road.

113

草の戸の草に住蚊も有ときけ

kusa no to no kusa ni juu ka mo ari to kike

I can hear
the mosquitoes living
in the thatch of my humble hut.

虫ぼしや片山里の松魚節

mushiboshi ya katayamazato no matsuobushi

Summer airing day![105]
In a remote mountain village –
dried bonito[106].

水練の師は敷草のすゞみ哉

suiren no shi wa shikigusa no suzumi kana

He's a master of swimming!
Cooling off
after applying mulch[107].

---

[105] A day to remove moisture from all one's belongings after the rainy season. The key thing was letting a dry breeze blow through the house to which items would be taken out and exposed.

[106] Used in betrothal gifts. The name (pine fish rings) comes from the fact that the cut end of the bonito resembles the annual rings of a pine tree which carries the wish of giving birth and raising healthy and long-lived children.

[107] Laying down straw around one's crops that eventually turns to mulch.

前鬼にも呑せて行や香需散

zenki ni mo nomesete yuku ya kouju kana

> At Zenki[108]
>> taking some as I travel along –
>>> mosla punctulata[109].

病で死ぬ人を感ずる暑哉

yande shinu hito o kanzuru atsusa kana

> Feeling the heat –
>> people getting sick
>>> and dying.

色濃くも藍の干上るあつさかな

irokoku mo ai no hiagaru atsusa kana

> They're dark –
>> the indigo plants
>>> drying out in the heat.

---

[108] An area in Nara Prefecture near Kyoto.
[109] A genus of plants in the family Lamiaceae. It is used in herbal medicine and Taigi I assume is drinking a concoction.

世の外に身をゆるめゐる暑かな
yo no soto ni mi o yurume iru atsui kana

    Detached from the world
       I take it easy
         in the heat.

めでたきも女は髪の暑サ哉
medetaki mo onna wa kami no atsusa kana

    In spite of the heat[110]
       the woman
         is still happy.

朝寐しておのれ悔しき暑さ哉
asane shite onore kuyashiki atsusa kana

    Sleeping in, in the morning,
       I'm so annoyed at myself –
         the heat!

---

[110] Literally "hot hair."

有侘て這ふて出けむかたつぶり

ari wabite hauteide kemu katatsuburi

It's worried –
    crawling out from the smoke,
        a snail!

蚊屋釣てくるゝ友あり草の庵

kaya tsurite kureru tomo ari kusa no io

A friend gives me
    a mosquito net for fishing
        at the thatched hut!

引入て夢見顔也かたつぶり

hikiirete yumemi gao nari katatsuburi

Withdrawn inside its shell,
    I dream of its face –
        the snail!

水の中へ銭遣りけらし心太
mizu no naka e zenizukari kerashi tokoroten

> The money I spent,
>> into the water –
>>> gelidium jelly[111].

怠ぬあゆみおそろしかたつぶり
darukunu ayumi osoroshi katatsuburi

> Frightened,
>> it briskly moves along –
>>> the snail.

扇とる手へもてなしのうちは哉
ougi toru te e motenashi no uchiwa kana

> Taking up the folding fan
>> in my hand
>>> rather than the non-folding one.

---

[111] Made of agar from red algae. It is prepared by soaking and boiling in water. Used in preparing various delicacies.

雷止んで太平簫ひく涼かな

rai yande taiheishou hiku suzumi kana

> The thunderstorm is over –
>> the charumera[112] is played
>>> in the coolness.

蠅をうつ首も厳しや関の人

hae o utsu kubi mo kibishi ya seki no hito

> Unsparingly
>> he swats the fly on his neck –
>>> the barrier guard.[113]

風呂布のつゝむに余る団かな

furo nuno no tsutsumu ni amaru dan kana

> There's too many people!
>> I wrap the bath cloth
>>> around me.

---

[112] A double-reed instrument that later gave rise to the oboe. It was often played by *ramen* vendors. The Japanese used here is the alternative, *taiheishou*.

[113] Blyth has a variant with *oto* (sound) instead of *kubi* (neck) – Blyth, *Haiku* v3, p. 201.

蚊帳ごしは柄から参らすうちはかな

kaya goshi wa e kara mairasu uchiwa kana

Through the mosquito net
I draw in the fan
by its handle.

夜を寐ぬと見ゆる歩みや蝸牛

yo o nenu to miyuru ayumi ya katatsumuri

Not sleeping at night
I see it sliding along –
the snail!

あふぎける団を腕に敷寐かな

ougi keru dan o ude ni shiki ne kana

As I lie down on the futon
and cover my arms,
I kick a fan.

ゆふだちや落馬もふせぐ旅の笠
yuudachi ya rakuba mo fusegu tabi no kasa

> Evening shower!
>> Preventing it from falling from the horse,
>>> the traveller's bamboo hat.

いで来たる硯の蝿の一つかみ
idekitaru suzuri no hae no hitotsukami

> Coming out
>> from the inkstone –
>>> a handful of flies!

書棄し歌もこし折うちは哉
sho sushi uta mo koshi ori uchiwa kana

> Putting down
>> a book of ancient verse[114] –
>>> it's time for the fan!

---

[114] Almost certainly *tanka* (*waka*).

盗人に出合ふ狐や瓜ばたけ

nusubito ni deau kitsune ya uribatake

    The thief
        bumped into a fox –
            in the melon field!

姫顔に生し立けむ瓜ばたけ

himegao ni ooshitatsu kemu uribatake

    Little faces
        growing through the haze –
            the melon field!

列立て火影行鵜や夜の水

retsuritsute hokage gyou u ya yoru no mizu

    In a row by firelight,
        cormorants[115] taking off –
            evening waters.

---

[115]   These would be cormorants on a fishing boat at night.

さつき咲庭や岩根の黴ながら

satsuki saki niwa ya iwane no kabinagara

> Azaleas bloom
>> in the garden
>>> while mould covers the rocks.

なぐさめて粽解なり母の前

nagusamete chimaki kai nari haha no mae

> It's comforting –
>> watching mother
>>> unwrap the *chimaki*[116].

舟梁に細きぬれ身やあら鵜共

funabari ni hosoki nure mi ya ara udomo

> On the boat's beam
>> with their thin, wet bodies –
>>> ah, the cormorants!

---

[116] Glutinous rice stuffed with different fillings and wrapped in bamboo leaves.

筍のすへ筍や丈あまり

takenoko no sue takenoko ya take amari

> The bamboo shoots,
>> the tips of the bamboo shoots,
>>> are very long!¹¹⁷

白罌粟や片山里の朦の中

shirokeshi ya katayamazato no mou no naka

> White poppies!
>> In the dim moonlight
>>> of a remote mountain village.

牡丹一輪筒に傾く日数かな

botan ichirin tsutsu ni katamuku hikasu kana

> The single peony in the vase¹¹⁸
>> has been drooping
>>> for a number of days¹¹⁹.

---

[117] Once more Taigi is playing with the sounds in this one.
[118] A cylindrical vase to be precise.
[119] The peony starts to droop as the flower is so large and heavy (thanks to Blyth for this).

124

切る人やうけとる人や燕子花
hiru hito ya uketoru hito ya kakitsubata

> Some people cut them,
>   then others receive them –
>   rabbit-ear iris.

こゝろほど牡丹の撓む日数かな
kokoro hodo botan no tawamu hikazu kana

> For several days
>   the peony's been drooping
>   as has my heart.

低く居て富貴をたもつ牡丹哉
hikuku ite fuuki o tamotsu botan kana

> Drooping
>   but still classy[120] –
>   the peony!

---

[120] Literally "wealth and status" but also an epithet for the peony.

碓の幕にかくる〽祭かな
usu no maku ni kakureru matsuri kana

Hidden under the cover
of the rice-pounding tub[121] –
festive delicacies!

門へ来し花屋にみせるぼたん哉
mon e kishi hanaya ni miseru botan kana

Arriving at the gate
of the florist,
with her display of peonies.

妾が家は江の西にあり菰粽
mekake ga ie wa e no nishi ni ari komochimaki

At the concubine's house
on the west side of the river
there is *komo chimaki*[122].

---

[121] Used to pound rice with various ingredients to make *mochi* (rice cake).
[122] Glutinous rice stuffed with different fillings and in this case, wrapped in Manchurian wild rice (*makomo*) leaves. It is traditionally served on Boy's Day on the 5th day of the fifth month, although bamboo leaves are now used.

妾人にくれし夜ほとゝぎす
shoujin ni kureshi yoru hototogisu

    In the darkening evening
       at the concubine's –
          the cuckoo!

下手乗せて馬もあそぶや藤の森
heta nosete uma mo asobu ya fujinomori

    Clumsily getting on the horse,
       I still enjoy myself –
          Fujinomori Shrine![123]

武士の子の眠さも堪る照射かな
bushi no ko no nemusa mo tamaru tomoshi kana

    The sleepy
       samurai children –
          putting up with the lanterns!

---

[123] This shrine in Kyoto is associated with prayers for horses (both health and racing). It is very ancient and may be where the Boy's (Children's) Festival originated. Also known as Fujimori Shrine.

127

しらで猶余所に聞なす水鶏かな

shira de nao yoso ni kikunasu kuina kana

I know of another instance
   of one sounding human[124] –
      the water rail!

蚊屋釣て豊に安し住る民

kaya tsurite yutaka ni yasushi juuru min

The people living
   peacefully in prosperity –
      fishing with mosquito nets!

蓴菜やしるよししける水所

junsai ya shiru yoshi shikeru mizu tokoro

Water shield![125]
   I know why it's moist –
      it's a watery place!

---

[124] Usually this relates to a bird's call sounding like Japanese words but here it
       has a broader meaning. The water rail was known to make a call like a
       knock at the door. This motif was common in haiku (e.g. Basho).
[125] An aquatic plant.

蚊屋釣や夜学を好む真ッ裸
kaya tsuri ya yagaku o konomu mappadaka

    Fishing with a mosquito net –
        Being naked
            I prefer learning in the evening!

蚊屋くゞる今更老が不調法
kaya kuguru imasara oi ga buchouhou

    The old man
        finally enters the mosquito net –
            he was so clumsy.

つれづれに水風呂たくや五月雨
tsurezure ni suifuro taku ya satsukiame

    Waiting for the bath to heat up
        is so tiresome –
            Fifth Month rain!

帰来る夫の咽ぶ蚊やりかな
kikuru otto no musebu kayari kana

The husband returning home
    is choking
        on the mosquito repellent!

やさしやな田を植るにも母の側
yasashi ya na ta o ueru ni mo haha no soba

It's easy!
    Planting rice in the fields
        beside mother.

めかしさよ夏書を忍ぶ後口向
mekashisa yo gegaki o shinobu ushiromuki

All dressed up!
    Hiding away the sutras
        I turn my back on them.

抽てむめ勝けりな寺若衆
hikite mume katsu keri na terawakashu

> Taking
>   the plum he won –
>   the temple acolyte[126].

青梅や女のすなる飯の菜
aoume ya onna no sunaru meshi no sai

> The unripe plums!
>   She uses them
>   in the side dish of rice.

さみだれの漏て出て行庵かな
samidare no morite deteiku iori kana

> Fifth Month rain!
>   Water leaking out
>   from my hut.

---

[126]   A boy who assisted the chief priest at a temple but also often a sexual
partner, even dressed up in female attire.

みじか夜や今朝関守のふくれ面

mijikayo ya kesa sekimori no fukurezura

The short summer night!
This morning, the barrier guard
looks sullen.

青梅のにほひ侘しくもなかりけり

aoume no nioi wabishiku mo nakarikeri

There's nothing worse
than the smell
of unripe plums.

傘焼し其日も来けり�が雨

kasa yasshi so hi mo kikeri tora ga ame

When it fell that day
it even burned umbrellas –
Tora's rain[127].

---

[127] Rain on the 28th day of the fifth month is related to the tears of sorrow shed by Tora Gozen, the lover of one of the Soga brothers killed that day. "Burning" tears I presume.

高麗人の旅の厠や夏木立
komaudo no tabi no kawaya ya natsukodachi

    The toilet of the traveller
        from Korea –
            a summer grove.

子子やてる日に乾く根なし水
boufura ya teru hi ni kawaku nenashi mizu

    Mosquito larvae!
        The standing water dries up
            on a sunny day.

甘き香は何の花ぞも夏木立
amaki ka wa nan no hana zo mo natsukodachi

    A sweet fragrance!
        What blossom is that
            in the summer grove?

夜渡る川のめあてや夏木立

yoru wataru kawa no meate ya natsukodachi

> A landmark
>> for crossing the river at night –
>>> the summer grove.

余花もあらむ子に教へ行神路山

yoka mo aramu ko ni oshie yuku kamijiyama

> I'd like to see late blossoms[128]
>> as I pass through Kamijiyama[129]
>>> to teach some children.

西風の若葉をしほるしなへかな

nishikaze no wakaba o shioru shinae kana

> The young leaves
>> are bent back
>>> in the west wind.

---

[128] This usually refers to cherry blossoms.
[129] A mountainous area near Ise and the Ise Shrine.

かしこげに着て出て寒き袷哉
kashikoge ni kite dete samuki awase kana

She's uses her head –
   going out in a lined kimono
      when it's cold!

苗代や日あらで又も通る路
nawashiro ya hi ara de mata mo touru michi

The rice plant nursery!
   Going down the road
      once more the sun is out.

いとほしい痩子の裾や更衣
ito hoshii yasego no suso ya koromogae

The hem of the thin child's garment
   needs mending –
      Change of Clothes Day[130].

---

[130]   On the 1st day of the fourth lunar month one changed to summer clothes.

物がたき老の化粧や衣更

monogataki oi no keshou ya koromogae

    The prudent old woman
        all made up –
            Change of Clothes Day!

まづ活けて返事誰書くなり蓮のもと

mazu ikete henji kaku nari hasu no moto

    First I arrange them,
        then write my reply
            under the lotus blossoms.

廻國の笈にさしゆく團扇哉

kaikoku no oi ni sashi yuku uchiwa kana

    I slide my slim
        folding fan
            into my pilgrim's box[131].

---

[131]   A wooden box that pilgrims carried on their back to hold their belongings, including religious items.

夕立のすは来る音よ森の上
yuudachi no suwa kuru oto yo mori no ue

> Startlingly,
>> the patter of a sudden evening shower
>>> sounds atop the forest.

行く女袷着すや憎きまで
iku onna awase kinasu ya nikuki made

> The woman traveller
>> is wearing her lined kimono –
>>> isn't **that** just lovely?

もとの水にあらぬしかけや心太
moto no mizu ni aranu shikake ya tokoroten

> The water in the rinsing device[132]
>> is never the same –
>>> gelidium jelly.

---

[132] Water flows through a device to cool the jelly. Thanks to Blyth, *History of Haiku* v1, p. 307 for the explanation here.

昼寝して手の動きやむ團扇かな
hirune shite te no ugokiyamu uchiwa kana

An afternoon nap –
my hand stops moving
the fan.

飛ぶ蛍あれと言はんもひとりかな
tobu hotaru are to iwan mo hitori kana

"Ah, a firefly!"
But I couldn't say it –
I was alone.

しづまれば流るる足や水馬
shizumareba nagaruru ashi ya mizusumashi

When it stops,
it floats away on its legs –
the whirligig!

芍薬の蕊の湧きたつ日向哉

shakuyaku no zui no wakitatsu hinata kana

> The stamens and pistil
> > of the Chinese peony
> > > spring out in the sunlight!

飲きりし旅の日数や香薷散

nomikiri shi tabi no hi kazu ya koujusan

> I finished taking it all,
> > having travelled many days –
> > > medicine for the heat![133]

白き花のこぼれてもあり番椒

shiroki hana no koborete mo ari banshou

> Their white blossoms
> > scattering –
> > > the pepper plant[134].

---

[133] *Elsholtzia ciliata*, or Vietnamese balm, which can induce sweating.
[134] *Capsicum annuum*, specifically shishito pepper.

新茶煮る暁おきや仏生会

shincha niru akatsuki oki ya busshoue

> The season's first tea simmers
> as I awake at dawn –
> Buddha's Birthday[135] celebration!

穂にむせぶ咳もさはがしむぎの秋

ho ni musebu seki mo sa hagashi mugi no aki

> Choking in ears of grain,
> raucously coughing –
> ripened barley![136]

深山路を出抜てあかし麦の秋

miyamaji o denukete akashi mugi no aki

> Passing along
> a remote mountain road
> I see fields of ripened barley!

---

[135] 8th day of the fourth lunar month.
[136] Literally "autumn barley" but in fact it means when barley has ripened in early summer.

麦秋や馬に出て行馬鹿息子
bakushuu ya uma ni deteiku baka musuko

    The wheat harvest!
      The stupid son
         leaves behind the horse.

Autumn

馴て出る鼠のつらや小夜ぎぬた

narete deru nezumi no tsura ya sayokinuta

> I'm getting used to the faces
> of the mice peeking out –
>   pounding of the fulling block[137] at night.

や〻あつて水に生たるもみぢ哉

yaya atsute mizu ni namataru momiji kana

> Ow! In the hot water
> they've sprouted –
>   red leaves of autumn!

暁の籠をぬけけんむしの声

akatsuki no kago o nuke ken mushi no koe

> The call of the insect
> escaping from its cage
>   at dawn.

---

[137] A wooden block to beat clothes and cloth to clean and thicken them.

寒きとて寝る人もあり暮の秋

samuki tote neru hito mo ari kure no aki

> The end of autumn –
>> people can still sleep
>>> even though it's cold.

いく浦のきぬたや聞てかがり船

iku ura no kinuta ya kiite kagaribune

> I go to the fulling blocks[138]
>> by the bay
>>> and listen to the bonfire boats[139].

中菊や地に這ふばかり閑なる

chuugiku ya ji ni hau bakari shizuka naru

> Edo chrysanthemums[140]
>> creeping along the ground –
>>> all is now tranquil.

---

[138] A wooden block to beat clothes and cloth to clean and thicken them.

[139] Boats that go along with the fishing fleet to illuminate the area or startle the fish so they are easily caught in nets.

[140] A medium-flowered chrysanthemum popular in the Edo period.

中入に見まふ和尚や茸がり
nakairi ni mi mau oshou ya kinokogari

Entering the mountains
I see Buddhist monks dancing[141] –
hunting for mushrooms.

おもはずもよそに更しぬ十三夜
omowazu mo yoso ni fukashinu juusanya

Though my mind was elsewhere,
it's not too late –
thirteenth night moon viewing[142].

しづめたるきくの節句の匂ひ哉
shizumetaru kiku no sekku no nioi kana

It's calming –
the scent
at the Chrysanthemum Festival[143].

---

[141] *Mau* implying a circular or whirling dance.
[142] A special moon viewing day on the 13th day of the ninth lunar month.
[143] Held the 9th day of the ninth lunar month.

あさ寒や旅の宿たつ人の声

asasamu ya tabi no yado tatsu hito no koe

    The morning cold!
       At the traveller's inn
          the voices of people leaving.

朝市や通かゝりてけふの菊

asaichi ya toori kakarite kyou no kiku

    The morning market!
       Strung up by the road
          today's chrysanthemums.

名月の昼迄大工遣ひかな

meigetsu no hiru made daiku tsukai kana

    Until the day
       of the harvest moon[144]
          carpenters busy at work.

---

[144] 15th day of the eighth lunar month. The carpenters are building moon-viewing platforms or towers I presume.

147

くさの戸の用意おかしや菊の酒

kusa no to no youi okashi ya kiku no sake

> Preparing sweets
>> for my humble dwelling –
>>> chrysanthemum wine[145].

田舎から柿くれにけり十三夜

inaka kara kaki kure ni keri juusanya

> At dusk
>> persimmons from the countryside –
>>> thirteenth night moon viewing[146].

十三夜月はみるやととなりから

juusanya tsuki wa miru ya to tonari kara

> Gazing
>> at the thirteenth night moon
>>> from my neighbour's.

---

[145] For the 9th day of the ninth month celebrations (Chrysanthemum Festival).
[146] A special moon viewing day on the 13th day of the ninth lunar month.

いなづまや雨雲わかるやみのそら

inazuma ya amagumo wakaru yami no sora

A flash of lightning!
  I can make out the rain clouds
      in the dark sky.

名月や船なき磯の岩づたひ

meigetsu ya fune naki iso no iwazutai

The harvest moon![147]
  Going from rock to rock on the beach –
      no boats in sight.

聞はづす声につゞくや鹿の声

kiku hazusu koe ni tsuzuku ya shika no koe

I missed it at first
  but the sound continued –
      the cry of the deer.

---

[147] The 15th day of the eighth month.

日は竹に落て人なし小鳥網

nichi wa take ni ote hito nashi kotoriami

> During the day, in the bamboo,
> > no one tripped over
> > > the small bird trap[148].

降れても行や月見の泊客

furete mo yuki ya tsukimi no tomarikyaku

> It's still raining –
> > travellers and those out moon viewing,
> > > overnight guests at the inn.

稲妻の無き日は空のなつかしき

inazuma no naki hi wa sora no natsukashiki

> Lightning and no sun –
> > I'm yearning
> > > for the clear blue sky[149].

---

[148] A net trap.
[149] The original just says "sky."

芋むしはいものそよぎにみえにけり
imo mushi wa imo no soyogi ni mie ni keri

> The potato bug
>   was seen stirring
>   on the potato.

いなづまやよわりよわりて雲の果
inazuma ya yowari yowarite kumo no hate

> Lightning!
>   Weakening, weakening –
>   the clouds disperse.

いなづまのこもりてみゆれ草の原
inazuma no komorite mi yure kusa no hara

> A flash of lightning!
>   Staying indoors
>   I see the plants swaying in the field.

もる〻香や蘭も覆の紙一重

moreru ka ya ran mo kutsugae no kami hitoe

    The scent comes through!
        Even covering the orchid
            with a layer of paper.

猪の庭ふむ音や木の実ふる

inoshishi no niwa fumu oto ya konomi furu

    The sound of a pig
        treading in the garden –
            fallen fruit!

手折てははなはだ長し女郎花

taotte wa hanahada nagashi ominaeshi

    Plucking it,
        it's really long –
            golden lace!

待宵やくるゝにはやき家の奥
matsuyoi ya kureru ni hayaki ie no oku

Waiting for tomorrow's harvest moon[150]
   inside my house
      wishing it would hurry up and come!

鬼灯や物うちかこつ口のうち
hoozuki ya monouchi kakotsu kuchi no uchi

The groundcherry[151] –
   the tip of my sword sliced it off
      so now it's in my mouth!

鉢の子ににえたつ粥や今年米
hachi no ko ni nietatsu kayu ya kotoshigome

In the children's bowls,
   rice porridge, just come to a boil –
      this year's rice[152]!

---

[150] It's on the night of the 14th day of the eight month that he is waiting.

[151] *Alkekengi officinarum* also known as the Chinese lantern plant. It's attractive fruit is edible but not a delicacy and the leaves are poisonous. Notice that this haiku has three "*uchi*" sounds in it.

[152] Rice just harvested that autumn.

着物のうせてわめくや辻角力

kimono no usete wameku ya tsujizumou

> Ranting about
>> my missing kimono –
>>> sumo wrestling at town square.

はつ雁やこゝろつもりの下リ所

hatsugan ya kokorozumori no ori tokoro

> The geese have arrived!
>> They've planned on coming
>>> for a long time.

さはがしき露の栖やくつわ虫

sawagashiki tsuyu no sumika ya kutsuwamushi

> It's noisy!
>> The katydids[153]
>>> in their dewy home.

---

[153] Katydids are nocturnal.

154

夜の間の露ゆりすふる広葉哉
yoru no kan no tsuyu yurisu furu hiroba kana

During the night
    dew falls
        from the swaying broad leaves.

はつ鴈や夜は目の行ものゝ隅
hatsugan ya yoru wa me no iku mono no sumi

The geese have arrived!
    In the evening I go to watch them
        in their V-formation.

吹倒す起す吹るゝ案山子かな
fukitaosu okosu fukareru kakashi kana

It's blown down and rises up,
    then blown down again –
        the scarecrow!

片足は踏とゞまるやきりぎりす

kataashi wa fumitodomaru ya kirigirisu

> One leg –
>> it's standing on one leg!
>>> the katydid!

よひやみや門に稚き踊声

yoiyami ya mon ni yayakoki odori koe

> The evening darkness[154] –
>> voices of the child dancers
>>> at the gate.

朝さむく蝿のわたるや竈の松

asa samuku hae no wataru ya kudo no matsu

> Cold morning,
>> flies buzzing about –
>>> pine[155] firewood in the hearth.

---

[154] The darkness before the moon appears on the 16th to 20th of the eight month.
[155] There could be a pun on *matsu* (homonym for "pine" and "wait") here: waiting for it to heat up.

狼のまつりか狂ふ牧の駒

ookami no matsuri ka kuruu maki no koma

The Wolf Festival[156] –
   the ponies in the pasture
      go crazy!

刀豆やのたりと下る花まぢり

natamame ya no tarito kudaru hana majiri

Slowly falling blossoms
   mingle with
      the sword beans[157].

はつ秋や団扇の風をひいた人

hatsuaki ya uchiwa no kaze o hiita hito

The beginning of autumn!
   The breeze from my fan
      draws that person near.

---

[156] Wolves were revered as messengers of the Shinto gods, as well helping control herbivores in an agricultural society.

[157] *Canavalia gladiata.*

夕されや軒の烟草に野分ふく

yuusare ya noki no tabako ni nowaki fuku

In the evening, a late autumn wind
   blows smoke from my pipe
      over the eaves.

たま祭持仏に残す阿弥陀かな

tamamatsuri jibutsu ni nokosu amida kana

During the Festival of the Dead[158],
   Amida
      left his Buddha statue.

駕に居て挑灯もつやはつ嵐

kago ni ite chouchin motsu ya hatsuarashi

I'm sitting in a palanquin
   holding a lantern –
      early autumn gale.

---

[158] Tama Matsuri, another appellation for Bon Matsuri (Festival), when spirits
   return to their birthplace and are revered. Literally, "soul festival."

初恋や燈籠によする顔と顔
hatsukoi ya tourou ni yosuru kao to kao

> First love –
>> getting close by the lantern,
>>> face to face.

めでたくも作り出けり芋の丈
medetaku mo tsukuri ide keri imo no take

> It's looks promising,
>> shooting right up –
>>> the height of the taro plant.

土照りて裂るや草の生ひながら
tsuchi terite sakeru ya kusa no oinagara

> In the dry weather,
>> the cracked earth –
>>> plants still growing.

水打て露こしらへる門辺哉

mizuuchite tsuyu koshiraeru monhe kana

> Watering
>   by the gate –
>   I've created dew!

眼ざましにみる背戸ながら今朝の露

mezamashi ni miru sedonagara kesa no tsuyu

> Waking up,
>   I see out the back door,
>   morning dew.

船よせて見れば柳のちる日かな

fune yosete mireba yanagi no chiru hi kana

> As I watch the boat approaching,
>   willow leaves fall and scatter
>   in the sunlight.

行秋や抱けば身に添ふ膝頭
yukuaki ya idakeba mi ni sou hizagashira

    Departing autumn!
       Hugging my knees
          feels good.

塚に蕣さきぬくれの秋
chirizuka ni asagao sakinu kure no aki

    In the rubbish heap,
       morning glories blooming –
         the end of autumn.

寐て起て長き夜にすむひとり哉
nete okite nagakiyo ni sumu hitori kana

    Lying in bed awake –
      all alone
        during the long autumn night.

長き夜や夢想さらりと忘れける
nagakiyo ya musou sarari to wasure keru

> The long autumn night –
>> forgetting
>>> my refreshing dream.

長きよや余所に寝覚し酒の酔
nagakiyo ya yoso ni nezame shi sake no yoi

> The long autumn night –
>> Waking up in a strange place
>>> drunk on *sake!*

落る日や北に雨もつ暮の秋
ochiru hi ya kita ni ame motsu kure no aki

> The setting sun!
>> The rain is holding in the north –
>>> the end of autumn.

壁つゞる傾城町やくれのあき

kabe tsuzuru keiseimachi ya kure no aki

Patching the walls
of the pleasure quarters –
the end of autumn.

あきの夜や自問自答の気の弱

aki no yo ya jimonjitou no ki no yowari

Autumn evening –
answering my own questions
without any conviction.

永き夜を半分酒に遣ひけり

nagakiyo o hanbun sake ni tsukai keri

The long autumn night –
I spent half of it
drinking *sake*.

夜の香や烟草寐せ置庭の隅
yoru no ka ya tabako nese oku niwa no sumi

A fragrant evening –
    lying in a corner of the garden
        smoking my pipe.

小山田の水落す日やしたりがほ
oyamada no mizu otosu hi ya shitarigao

The sun sets
    over the waters of a mountain rice field –
        feeling ecstatic!

身ひとつをよせる籬や種ふくべ
mi hitotsu o yoseru magaki ya tane fukube

Alone
    I approach the fence –
        gourds growing.

新米のもたるゝ腹や穀潰し

shinmai no motareru hara ya gokutsubushi

> The new rice growing,
>   brushing my belly –
>   just loafing.

薬掘蝮も提てもどりけり

kusurihori mamushi mo sagete modori keri

> Gathering medicinal herbs –
>   carrying back
>   a pit viper[159] too!

迷ひ出る道の薮根の照葉かな

mayoi deru michi no yabu ne no teriha kana

> Leaving the road,
>   I'm lost in a thicket
>   where autumn leaves gleam.

---

[159]   A Japanese pit viper (mamushi).

口を切る瓢や禅のかの刀

kuchi o kiru hisago ya zen no ka no katana

> I cut open
> the bottle gourd
> with an excellent Zen blade.

かぶり欠く柿の渋さや十が十

kaburi kaku kaki no shibusa ya juu ga juu

> Break open an astringent persimmon[160]
> and you're covered with juice –
> for sure[161]!

関越て亦柿かぶる袂かな

seki koshite mata kaki kaburu tamoto kana

> Crossing the barrier gate,
> once more my sleeves
> covered with persimmon juice!

---

[160] There are two varieties of persimmons in Japan, the native sweet kind and the astringent kind originally from China.

[161] Literally "10 out of 10" meaning completely or certainly. The sound in Japanese of this haiku should be noted.

166

残る葉と染かはす柿や二ッ三ッ

nokoru ha to some kawasu kaki ya futatsu mitsu

> The remaining leaves,
>> colours mingled with the persimmons –
>>> two or three.

柿売の旅寐は寒し柿の側

kakiuri no tabine wa samushi kaki no soba

> On a trip to sell persimmons
>> a chilly sleep –
>>> next to the persimmons!

空遠く声あはせ行小鳥哉

sora touku koe awase yuku kotori kana

> In the distant sky,
>> as I go along,
>>> the cries of small birds.

鉄槌に女や嬲るうちもみぢ
tetsu uchi ni onna ya naburu uchi momiji

    The women with the iron hammer
       makes fun
          striking the autumn leaves.

青き葉の吹れ残るや綿畠
aoki ha no fukare nokoru ya watahatake

    Only the green leaves
       blown by the wind remain –
          fields of cotton.

引けば寄蔦や梢のこゝかしこ
hikeba yose tsuta ya kozue no koko kashiko

    If you pull the ivy close
       the treetops up there
          will be down here.

夜に入ば灯のもる壁や蔦かづら
yo ni ireba hi no moru kabe ya tsuta kazura

As evening commences
    light leaks out from the shutters –
        ivy and vines.

露を見る我尸や草の中
tsuyu o miru ware shikabane ya kusa no naka

I'm like a corpse,
    staring at the dew –
        amidst the plants.

町庭のこゝろに足るやうす紅葉
machi niwa no kokoro ni taru ya usu momiji

A garden in town
    suffices the heart –
        light autumn colours.

旅人や夜寒問合ふねぶた声

tabibito ya yosamu toiau nebutagoe

Travellers!
　　Asking about the evening cold
　　　　in sleepy voices.

舟曳のふねへ来ていふ夜寒哉

funehiki no fune e kite iu yosamu kana

Calling the boat puller
　　to come to my boat –
　　　　a cold evening.

椽端の濡てわびしやあきの雨

enbana no nurete wabishi ya aki no ame

The edge of the porch[162] is getting wet.
　　How dreary –
　　　　autumn showers.

---

[162]　The characters here seem to be conflated with 縁端. Both Soseki and Shiki render them as *enbana*. I have followed suit. The porch or *engawa* is a wooden structure running around a traditional Japanese home.

水瓶へ鼠の落し夜さむかな

mizugame e nezumi no otoshi yosamu kana

> A mouse fell
>> in the water jug –
>>> a cold evening!

やゝ老て初子育る夜寒かな

yaya oi te hatsune sodateru yosamu kana

> I'm growing steadily older –
>> it's already the first day of the Rat[163]!
>>> A cold night.

茄子売揚屋が門やあきの雨

nasubiuri ageya ga mon ya aki no ame

> The eggplant seller
>> at the entrance of the brothel –
>>> autumn showers.

---

[163] The first day of the Rat (zodiacal day) in the month. Usually it refers to the New Year or eleventh month, but here the time is autumn. I have added the word "already" to emphasize the meaning.

菊の香や花屋が灯むせぶ程

kiku no ka ya hanaya ga akari musebu hodo

> The fragrance of the chrysanthemums!
> > The flower shop's lantern
> > > is extinguished.

泊居てきぬた打也尼の友

tomariite kinuta uchi nari ama no tomo

> Staying over,
> > she pounds the fulling block[164] –
> > > her friend, the nun.

剃て住法師が母のきぬた哉

sotte juu houshi ga haha no kinuta kana

> The monk gets his head shaved
> > as his mother
> > > pounds the fulling block.

---

[164]   A wooden block to beat clothes and cloth to clean and thicken them.

寐よといふ寝ざめの夫や小夜砧
ne yo to iu nezame no otto ya sayokinuta

    "Come to bed,"
        cries the sleepless husband –
            the pounding of the fulling block at night.

出女の垣間見らるゝきぬた哉
de onna no kama mirareru kinuta kana

    The unlicensed prostitute
        can be seen through a gap in the hedge
            pounding the fulling block.

夜あらしに吹細りたるかゞし哉
yoarashi ni fukihosoritaru kagashi kana

    The strong night wind
        rips right through it –
            the scarecrow.

おどり人も減し芝居や秋のくれ

odoribito mo heshi shibai ya aki no kure

> The number of dancers and plays
> > is decreasing –
> > > the end of autumn.

古畑の疇ありながら野菊かな

furuhata no une ari nagara nogiku kana

> Although there is a path
> > through the old field,
> > > it's all wild chrysanthemums.

朝露や菊の節句は町中も

asatsuyu ya kiku no sekku wa machi naka mo

> Morning dew!
> > The Chrysanthemum Festival[165]
> > > in the midst of the city too!

---

[165] On the 9th day of the ninth lunar month.

ひとり居や足の湯湧す秋のくれ

hitori i ya ashi no yu wakusu aki no kure

> At home alone!
>> Hot water wells up over my feet –
>>> the end of autumn.

夕露に蜂這入たる垣根哉

yuutsuyu ni hachi haiitaru kakine kana

> Bees fly
>> to the evening dew
>>> on the hedge.

泊問ふ船の法度や秋の暮

tomari tou fune no hatto ya aki no kure

Requesting mooring for boats
>> is prohibited –
>>> the end of autumn.

有侘て酒の稽古やあきの暮
yuu wabite sake no keiko ya aki no kure

Feeling lonely
I practice drinking *sake* –
the end of autumn.

菊の香や山路の旅籠奇麗也
kiku no ka ya yamaji no hatago kirei nari

The fragrance of chrysanthemums!
At the lovely inn
on the mountain road.

石榴喰ふ女かしこうほどきけり
zakuro kuu onna ka shikou hodoki keri

The woman
eating a pomegranate
trying to pull it apart.

旅人やきくの酒くむ昼休み

tabibito ya kiku no sake kumu hiruyasumi

    The traveller –
        serving him chrysanthemum *sake*
            at lunchtime.

菊の香やひとつ葉をかく手先にも

kiku no ka ya hitotsuba o kaku tesaki ni mo

    The fragrance of chrysanthemums!
        As well I pluck a single leaf
            with my fingers.

大根も葱もそこらや蕎麦の花

daikon mo negi mo sokora ya soba no hana

    Daikon[166] and green onions
        everywhere –
            buckwheat blossoms!

---

[166] Large white Japanese radishes.

灯の届かぬ庫裏やきりぎりす
akari no todokanu kuri ya kirigirisu

> No light reaches
>   the monastery kitchen –
>   a katydid!

うら枯ていよいよ赤しからす瓜
ura karete iyoiyo akashi karasuuri

> Their tips withering
>   more and more –
>   red crow gourds[167].

うかれ来て蚊屋外しけり月の友
ukare kite kaya soto shi keri tsuki no tomo

> They came floating by
>   outside the mosquito net –
>   companions of the moon!

---

[167] *Trichosanthes cucumeroides*. A red gourd that is bitter but edible.

萩活て置けり人のさはるまで

hagi ikite oku keri hito no sawaru made

> The bush clover
> was thriving there
> until someone tramped on it[168].

雪ふれば鹿のよる戸やきりぎりす

yuki fureba shika no yoru to ya kirigirisu

> When it snows
> the deer comes near the door –
> katydids.

後の月庭に化物作りけり

nochi no tsuki niwa ni bakemono tsukuri keri

> The thirteenth night moon[169]
> making phantoms
> in the garden!

---

[168] Literally, harmed or damaged it.
[169] A special moon viewing day on the 13th day of the ninth lunar month.

名月や花屋寐てゐる門の松

meigetsu ya hanaya neteiru kado no matsu

> Harvest moon![170]
>> The florist is sleeping
>>> by the pine gates[171].

みか月や膝へ影さす舟の中

mikazuki ya hiza e kage sasu fune no naka

> Crescent moon![172]
>> In the boat, it casts its light
>>> on my lap.

雨に来て泊とりたる月見かな

ame ni kite tomari toritaru tsukimi kana

> Coming in the rain,
>> looking for a place to stay –
>>> moon viewing!

---

[170] Full moon on the 15th of the eighth lunar month.
[171] Usually this means pine-decorated gates at New Year, but here there is a harvest moon.
[172] Literally "third day moon."

三日月の船行かたや西の海
mikagetsu no fune yukigata ya nishinoumi

> The ship sailing
> > under the crescent moon –
> > > the western sea.

来ると否端居や月のねだり者
kuru to ina hashii ya tsuki no nedari mono

> It won't come!
> > Sitting on the verandah
> > > pleading for the moon.

みそなはせ花野もうつる月の中
misonahase hanano mo utsuru tsuki no naka

> Look!
> > The flowers in the field[173]
> > > are reflecting the moonlight

---

[173] Particularly the seven autumn flowers: bush clover, miscanthus, kudzu, large pink, yellow-flowered valerian, boneset, and Chinese bellflower

181

おもはゆく鶉なく也蚊屋の外
omohayuku uzura naku nari kaya no soto

    The bashful quail
        cries
            outside of the mosquito net.

みか月やかたち作りてかつ寂し
mikazuki ya katachi tsukurite katsu sabishi

    The crescent moon!
        The shape of it
            is desolate.

身の秋やあつ燗好む胸赤し
mi no aki ya atsu kan konomu mune akashi

    I'm tired of autumn!
        I prefer hot *sake*
            and a reddened chest.

畠踏む似せ侍や小鳥狩

hatake fumu nise samurai ya kotorigari

Treading through fields,
   just like a samurai –
      the man hunting birds!

芋茎さく門賑しやひとの妻

zuiki saku mon nigiya shi ya hito no tsuma

Busily rooting up taro stems
   by the gate –
      his wife.

片店はさして餅売野分かな

kata mise wa sashite mochi uri nowaki kana

The side business –
   serving drinks and selling rice cakes.
      Late autumn storm[174].

183

みどり子に竹筒負せて生身魂
midorigo ni takezutsu fusete ikimitama

The infant is being carried
in a bamboo cylinder on her back –
Veneration for the Elderly Day![175]

渡し守舟流したる野分哉
watashimori fune nagashitaru nowaki kana

The ferryman's boat
is washed away –
late autumn storm.

蕣に垣ねさへなき住居かな
kibachisu ni kakine sae naki sumai kana

Hibiscus
by the house
without even a fence.

---

[175] *Ikimitama*: originally a meal during Bon time to honour the elderly. It evolved into Respect for the Aged Day, held the third Monday of September.

浅川の水も吹散る野分かな

asakawa no mizu mo fukichiru nowaki kana

> The waters of the Asakawa River[176]
>   are turbulent –
>   late autumn storm!

野分して樹々の葉も戸に流れけり

nowaki shite kigi no ha mo to ni nagare keri

> The late autumn storm
>   brought the leaves of many trees
>   flowing by our door.

荻吹や燃る浅間の荒残り

ogi fuku ya moeru asama no ara nokori

> Wind-blown silvergrass!
>   The devastation of the fire
>   on Mt. Asama[177].

---

[176] A tributary of the Tama River near Hino (west part of Tokyo).

[177] An active volcano on the border of Gunma and Nagano Prefectures. There was a major eruption in 1783, shortly after Taigi's death in 1771. I have assumed that the *asama* in the haiku refers to said volcano.

185

ものゝ葉に魚のまとふや下簗
mono no ha ni uo no matou ya kudariyana

> Amidst the leaves,
>   waiting for the fish –
>   the fish trap[178].

荻原に棄て有けり風の神
ogiwara ni sutete yuu keri kaze no kami

> Abandoned
>   to the field of silvergrass –
>   the Wind God[179].

簗をうつ漁翁がうそやことし限
yana o utsu gyoou ga uso ya kotoshi gen

> No way the old fisherman
>   smashed the fish trap –
>   this year anyway.[180]

---

[178] A *kudariyana,* which is a fairly large contraption.
[179] Fujin.
[180] Although fish trap (*yana*) is a summer seasonal word, this haiku was embedded with autumn pieces and there are variations on *yana* that are autumn.

秋さびしおぼえたる句を皆申す

aki sabishi oboetaru ku o mina mousu

Everyone says
to remember that autumn haiku
should be lonely and desolate.

鶏頭やはかなきあきを天窓勝

keitou ya hakanaki aki o atamagachi

Plumed cockscomb![181]
The champion head
of fleeting autumn.

鶏頭やひとつはそだつこぼれ種

keitou ya hitotsu wa sodatsu koboredane

Plumed cockscomb!
Just one,
growing there on its own.

---

[181] A flowering plant, *celosia argentea,* which is noted for its very bright colours.

187

静なる水や蜻蛉の尾に打も

shizuka naru mizu ya tonbo no o ni utsu mo

> The water becomes calm –
>> it was touched
>>> by a dragonfly's tail.

其葉さへ細きこゝろや女郎花

sono ha sae hosoki kokoro ya ominaeshi

> Even those leaves
>> catch one's attention –
>>> golden lace!

二里といひ一里ともいふ花野哉

ni ri to ii ichi ri to mo iu hanano kana

> Some say five miles,
>> some say two and a half miles –
>>> the field of flowers!

いなづまや舟幽霊の呼ふ声

inazuma ya funeyuurei no yobu koe

A flash of lightning!
The voice of sea phantoms
calling out.

送り火や顔覗あふ川むかひ

okuribi ya kao nozoki au kawa mukai

Obon bonfire[182] –
peeking at the face I see
across the river.

たま祭る料理帳有筆の跡

tamamatsuru ryourichou ari fude no ato

Festival of the Dead[183] –
the cookbook has been
marked up by the brush.

---

[182] A ceremonial bonfire to see off the spirits on the final night of Obon, the festival where ancestral spirits return and are honoured.

[183] Tama Matsuri, another appellation for Obon Matsuri (Festival), when spirits return to their birthplace Literally, "soul festival."

魂棚やぼた餅さめる秋の風

tamadana ya botamochi sameru aki no kaze

> The *tamadana*![184]
> > The adzuki *mochi*[185] has cooled down
> > > in the autumn breeze.

遺言の酒備へけり魂まつり

yuigon no sake sonae keri tamamatsuri

> Providing the *sake*
> > as my last request –
> > > Festival of the Dead!

懸乞の不機嫌みせそ魂祭

kakegoi no fukigen mise so tamamatsuri

> I'm not happy!
> > Seeing the bill collector
> > > at the Festival of the Dead.

---

[184] A shelf put up for offerings to one's ancestors.
[185] Rice cakes made with adzuki bean paste offered to Buddhist altars and
neighbours during the spring and autumn equinox.

笠ぬげば鹿の聞度夜とぞなる
kasa nugeba shika no kiku tabi yo to zo naru

> Taking off my bamboo hat at night
>> I could hear
>>> the bellowing deer.

つる草や蔓の先なる秋の風
tsurukusa ya tsuru no saki naru aki no kaze

> The vines –
>> their tips waving
>>> in an autumn breeze.

痩たるをかなしむ蘭の苔けり
yasetaru o kanashimu ran no tsubomi keri

> I felt down
>> at its barrenness,
>>> but the orchid has budded!

何もなし夫婦訪来し宿の秋

nani mo nashi fuufu tohikita shi yado no aki

> There are none –
>> no married couples
>>> visit the inn in autumn.

行先に都の塔や秋の空

yukisaki ni miyako no tou ya aki no sora

> The destination
>> far from the capital[186] –
>>> the autumn sky.

南無薬師薬の事もきく桔梗

namu yakushi kusuri no koto mo kiku kikyou

> Hail Yakushi Buddha![187]
>> And his efficacious medicine,
>>> the Chinese bellflower[188].

---

[186] Kyoto.
[187] The Medicine Buddha.
[188] Its roots are used for medicinal purposes. One of the seven autumn flowers.

夕立の晴行かたや揚灯炉

yuudachi no hare yuku kata ya age touro

> Travelling in clear weather,
>   a sudden shower!
>   I raise the lantern.

見かけ行ふもとの宿や高灯炉

mikake yuku fumoto no yado ya kou touro

> Travelling, I see an inn
>   at the foot of a mountain
>   with its lantern on high.

城内に踏ぬ庭あり轡むし

jounai ni fumanu niwa ari kutsuwamushi

> Within the castle grounds
>   I don't tread in the garden –
>   there are katydids![189]

---

[189] *Mecopoda nipponensis.* A different family of katydids from the *kirigirisu* usually found in haiku.

彼後家のうしろにおどる狐かな

kano goke no ushiro ni odoru kitsune kana

> Behind
>> the widow (you know who) –
>>> there's a fox dancing![190]

声きけば古き男や音頭取

koe kikeba furuki otoko ya ondotori

> Listening to the voice
>> of the elderly man –
>>> the lead singer!

さし鯖や袖とおぼしき振あはせ

sashisaba ya sode to oboshiki furu awase

> Mackerel *sashimi!*
>> Some appears to be swaying
>>> on the sleeves of my kimono.

---

[190] This is likely Bon Odori and the fox is, in fact, a man attracted to the woman (of dubious reputation).

家づとの京知顔やすまひとり

iezuto no kyou shirigao ya suma hitori

> Familiar faces
>> are my souvenirs of Kyoto –
>>> alone in Suma[191].

勝迦の旅人あやしや辻角力

katsu niga no tabibito ayashi ya tsujizumo

> The poor traveller
>> missed a great sight –
>>> roadside sumo wrestling[192].

山霧や宮を守護なす法螺の音

yamagiri ya miya o shugo nasu hora no oto

> Mountain mist!
>> Protecting the shrine
>>> the sound of conch shells[193].

---

[191] Famous in literature for its beach, now part of Kobe.
[192] An outdoor sumo match held in a vacant field or lot.
[193] Used to ward off wild animals.

裸身に夜半の鐘や辻相撲

rashin ni yahan no kane ya tsujizumou

    Midnight bells
        amidst the naked –
            roadside sumo wrestling.

明はなし寐た夜つもりぬ虫の声

mei wa nashi neta yo tsumorinu mushi no koe

    Not planning on sleeping tonight,
        not yet morning –
            the cry of insects.

初秋や障子さす夜とさゝぬよと

hatsuaki ya shouji sasu yo to sasanu yo to

    Early autumn –
        some *shoji*[194] shut for the night;
           some not shut for the night.

---

[194]   Sliding opaque paper partitions, in this case serving as windows.

引寄て蓮の露吸ふ汀かな

hikiyosete hasu no tsuyu suu migiwa kana

Drawing the lotus
　　towards me on shore
　　　　I sip the dew.

七夕や家中大かた妹と居す

tanabata ya kachuu ookata imo to isu

Tanabata![195]
　　My wife will probably
　　　　stay at home with her sister.

すゞしさのめでたかり鳧今朝の秋

suzushisa no medeta kari kamo kesa no aki

In the coolness,
　　admiring the ducks and geese –
　　　　an autumn morning.

---

[195] The festival celebrating the Herdsman and Weaver Girl (the stars Vega and Altair respectively). The Milky Way separates these lovers, and they are allowed to meet once a year on the seventh day of the seventh lunar month.

麦打に三女夫並ぶ栄へかな

mugiuchi ni mi otome narabu sakae kana

> In a row, three couples
> > threshing the barley –
> > > prosperity!

桃ありてますます白し雛の殿

momo arite masumasu shiroshi hina no tono

> There are more and more
> > white peaches –
> > > bird shit!

初秋や夕立長びく夜の雨

hatsuaki ya yodachi nagabiku yoru no ame

> The beginning of autumn!
> > The evening shower
> > > turned into a night of rain[196].

---

[196] The shower started on the last night of summer and continued into the first day of autumn.

初秋や浴みしあとの気のゆるみ
hatsuaki ya amishi ato no ki no yurumi

The beginning of autumn!
    After taking a bath
        feeling lethargic.

露を知ろ駕の寝覚や己が門
tsuyu o shiru kago no nezame ya ono ga kado

I notice the dew
    as I awake in the palanquin
        at my gate.

川霧や馬打入るる水の音
kawagiri ya uma uchiiruru mizu no oto

The river mist!
    Driving the horse in –
        the sound of water.

椿守と語りて月の名残かな

hashimori to katarite tsuki no nagori kana

> I chat
>> with the bridge guard
>>> under the waning moon[197].

今朝見ればこちら向たる案山子かな

kesa mireba kochira mukataru kakashi kana

> When I looked this morning,
>> it was facing this way!
>>> The scarecrow.

拝すとて烏帽子落すな司めし

haisu tote eboshi otosuna tsukasameshi

> When bowing,
>> don't let your hat[198] fall off –
>>> Official Appointment Day[199]!

---

[197] Specifically, the moon of the 13th night of the ninth lunar month.

[198] Namely, the *eboshi* hat used for official occasions.

[199] A special ceremony in autumn when new officials were appointed.

御命講の華のあるじや女形

omeikou no hana no aruji ya onnagata

> An offering of flowers
>> for Nichiren's memorial[200] –
>>> the *onnagata*[201].

Winter

とにかくにたらぬ日数や年忘

tonikaku ni taranu hikazu ya toshiwasure

    In any case
        a few days is not enough –
            forgetting the hardships of the year.

山ぶきのいはぬ色あり衣配

yamabuki no iwanu iro ari kinukuba

    The gift of clothes[202]
        has the same colour
            as the *yamabuki* yellow rose.

煤払のあら湯へ入る座頭かな

susuharai no ara yu e iru zatou kana

    The blind man
        enters the tub of hot water
            set aside for housecleaning day[203].

---

[202] Gifts of bright new clothes were presented to those close to one (usually relatives but servants too) in the twelfth lunar month for New Year's.

[203] The end of year cleaning done on the 13th day of the twelfth lunar month. All subsequent references to "housecleaning" or "sweeping out the soot" relate to this event.

眼に残る親の若さよ年の暮
me ni nokoru oya no waka sayo nen no kure

> End of the year –
>   the youth of the parents
>   remains in their eyes.

すゝはきや挑灯しらむ門の霜
susu waki ya chouchin shiramu mon no shimo

> Sweeping the soot out –
>   lighting up the folding lantern,
>   frost on the gate.

居風呂の底ふみぬくや年の暮
suefuro no soko fuminuku ya toshi no kure

> My foot went through
>   the bottom of the bathtub –
>   end of the year.

二階から土器投やすゝはらひ

nikai kara kawarake tou ya susuharai

Housecleaning day –
　earthenware was tossed
　　from the second floor!

年とるや帆柱の数ありそうみ

toshitoru ya hobashira no kazu ari soumi

Getting old!
　My body feels like
　　it's made up of ship masts.

わびしさや思ひたつ日を煤払

wabishisa ya omoi tatsu hi o susuharai

Feeling wretched –
　thinking about housecleaning
　　at sunrise.

すゝはきの中へ使やひねり文
susuhaki no naka e tsukai ya hineri bun

The messenger came
    while I was sweeping out soot
        with an elegant missive.

すゝ払てそろりとひらく持仏哉
susuharate sororito hiraku jibutsu kana

While housecleaning,
    very carefully
        taking out the Buddha statue.

としとしや煤よう掃て手向水
toshi toshi ya susu you hakute tougemizu

Year after year –
    sweeping out the soot;
        offering water to the *kami*[204] and ancestors.

狐なく霜夜にいづこ煤はらひ

kitsune naku shimoyo ni izuko susuharai

> While housecleaning,
>> outside in the frosty night,
>>> the cry of a fox.

餅つきやものゝ答へる深山寺

mochitsuki ya mono no kotaeru miyamadera

> Pounding *mochi*[205] –
>> responding,
>>> the distant mountain temple bell.

とし忘扨もひとには精進日

toshiwasure sate mo hito ni wa shoujinbi

> The end of year party[206]
>> falls on
>>> his day of abstinence[207].

---

[205] The glutinous rice to make Japanese rice cakes (*mochi*)
[206] New Year's Eve drinking party to "forget" the past year.
[207] A day of religious devotion to the *kami*, Buddha or one's ancestors.

208

俎板に這ふかとみゆる海鼠かな
manaita ni hau ka to miyuru namako kana

    I let the sea cucumber
        crawl across
            the cutting board.

道ばたの天秤棒や大根引
michibata no tenbinbou ya daikon hiki

    By the roadside
        with my carrying pole –
            pulling up *daikon*[208].

楼に哥舞伎の真似や煤払
takadono ni kabuki no mane ya susuharai

    In the courtesan's quarters
        mimicking kabuki –
            houseclearing day.

---

[208] A large white radish usually dried and pickled.

冬ごもる心の松の戸をほそめ

fuyugomoru kokoro no matsu no to o hosome

Confined inside by the winter –
I've narrowed the door
to my expectations[209].

霜の声ひとの鼾で寐ぬよ哉

shimo no koe hito no ibiki de nenu yo kana

I can't sleep!
The sound of the frost
and people snoring.

咲ている梅にもあふや寒念仏

sakiteiru ume ni mo au ya kan nenbutsu

I see again,
plum trees blossoming –
winter nembutsu[210].

---

[209] Literally "pine of the heart" but using the homonym (*matsu*) "waiting of the heart" (= "expectations"). I assume this is an amorous reference.
[210] Winter nembutsu: going to the mountains at dawn and chanting to Amida Buddha during 30 days of the coldest part of winter.

節季ぞろややむときはやむ物の声

sekkizoro ya yamu toki wa yamu mono no koe

> Twelfth month chanting[211] –
> > time stops,
> > > the sounds of nature cease.

対にしてかぞへて歩く鴛見哉

tai ni shite ka zo ete aruku oshi mi kana

> I watch the ducks
> > walking by
> > > in pairs.

髪おきやちと寒くとも肩車

kamioki ya chito samuku tomo kataguruma

> The children's hair ritual[212] –
> > it's a bit cold
> > > carried about on the shoulders.

---

[211] In the twelfth month (until about the 28th), men and women went around in small groups wearing special clothes and face covered, chanting festive songs and receiving alms of rice and money.

[212] A coming-of-age ritual held on the 15th day of the eleventh month when shaving a child's head ceased at age three. The child (boy or girl), would be carried on the father's shoulders at a Shinto shrine for the ritual. It survives symbolically today for girls as part of *shichi-go-san*.

髪おきやうしろ姿もみせ歩く

kamioki ya ushiro sugata mo mise aruku

> The children's hair ritual –
>> see them walking
>>> and the shape of their backs.

それとみる松の戸尻や茎の桶

sore to miru matsu no tojiri ya kuki no oke

> Looking over
>> by the pine *shoji*[213] jamb –
>>> a tub of pickles.

顔みせや状を出しあふ宇津の山

kao mise ya jou o dashiau utsunoyama

> Showing its face!
>> I come across the looming form
>>> of Mt. Utsu[214].

---

[213] A sliding door or partition in a Japanese house, usually with white
       translucent panels.
[214] Utsunoyama, on the old Tokkaido road at Okabe, near Shizuoka.

嫁みせに出て来る茶やの落ば哉

yome mise ni idekuru chaya no ochiba kana

    Coming out of the teahouse
        amidst the fallen leaves,
            presenting the bride.

かみ置やかゝへ相撲の肩の上

kamioki ya kaka e sumou no kata no ue

    The children's hair ritual[215]:
        on the shoulders of a sumo wrestler –
            people burst out laughing.

盃になるもの多し卵酒

sakazuki ni naru mono ooshi tamagozake

    Many *sake* eggnogs[216]
        can be drunk
            from a *sake* cup.

---

[215] A coming-of-age ritual held on the 15th day of the eleventh month when shaving a child's head ceased at age three. The child (boy or girl), would be carried on the father's shoulders at a Shinto shrine for the ritual. It survives symbolically today for girls as part of *shichi-go-san*.

[216] A heated drink made with eggs, sugar and eggnog. As it is not as strong as plain *sake*, it would take many tiny *sake* cups to get your fill.

手燈しの低き明りやくすり喰

shutou shi no hikuki akari ya kusurigui

> The hand lantern[217]'s
>> light is low –
>>> time for medicinal food[218]!

猟人の鉄鉋うつや雪の中

ryoujin no teppou utsu ya yuki no naka

> The hunter's rifle[219]
>> hits its target!
>>> Snow all around.

魚ぬすむ狐のぞくや網代守

uo nusumu kitsune nozoku ya ajiromori

> He spotted the fox
>> stealing the fish –
>>> the night watchman of the fishing grounds[220].

---

[217] A Buddhist practice of using oil (or a candle) in one's palm as a lamp.

[218] In winter, deer and boar flesh were consumed to make one strong against the harsh winter. The euphemism "medicinal food" was used.

[219] I have treated 鉄鉋 as a variant of 鉄砲 meaning "rifle."

[220] The watchman lit a fire and watched over the elaborate setup of fishing nets. A well-known one was located at Uji near Kyoto.

あるほどの水を入江の氷かな
aru hodo no mizu ɔ irie no kouri kana

The water
    in the cove
        is entirely frozen over.

木葉ちる風や戸をさす竈の前
konoha chiru kaze ya to o sasu kudo no mae

Fallen leaves blown by the wind –
    I close the door
        and sit before the hearth.

枯くさや薮根の椿落る迄
karekusa ya yabu ne no tsubaki ochiru made

The withered grass –
    camellias fall
        to the roots of the underbrush.

雪見とて出るや武士の馬に鞍

yukimi tote ideru ya bushi no uma ni kura

> Going out snow viewing
>> riding in the saddle
>>> of a samurai horse.

関守へ膳おくり来つゑびす講

sekimori e zen okuri kitsu webisukou

> The Ebisu festival[221] approaching
>> I send a meal
>>> to the barrier guard.

苞にする十の命や寒鷄卵

tsuto ni suru juu no inochi ya samu keiran

> Wrapped in straw,
>> ten lives –
>>> winter chicken eggs.

---

[221] A festival held the 20th day of the eleventh lunar month (and other dates) seeking the aid of Ebisu, the god of fisherman (and later, harvest and commercial success), for a prosperous fishing catch.

親も子も酔へばねる気よ卵酒
oya mo ko mo yoeba neru ki yo tamagozake

> Parents, and the children too,
>   if they get drunk, will feel like sleeping –
>   *sake* eggnog.

腰かけて紅葉みつらん炭俵
koshikakete momoji mitsuran sumidawara

> I sit down
>   on a sack of charcoal
>   awaiting the full fall colours[222].

寒菊や茂る葉末のはだれ雪
kangiku ya shigeru hazue no hadare yuki

> Winter chrysanthemums!
>   Snow falling
>   on the tips of the luxuriant leaves.

---

[222] This seems like an autumn haiku but the idea is: it's winter, the fall colours are over, but already I'm waiting for next year's.

217

かれ芦や鴨見なくせし鷹の声

kare ashi ya kamo minakuseshi taka no koe

The withered reeds –
  spying the ducks
    the hawk cries out.

水仙や茎みじかくと己が園

suisen ya kuki mijikaku to ora ga sono

Daffodils!
  The ones in my garden
    have short stems.

くらがりの柄杓にさはる氷かな

kuragari no hishaku ni sawaru kouri kana

Touching my dipper
  in the darkness –
    ice!

さむき夜や探れば窪き老が肩
samuki yo ya sagureba kuboki oi ga kata

    A cold night!
        Feeling around for hollows
            on my old shoulders.

寒ぎくや垣根つづきの庵の数
samugiku ya kakine tsuzuki no io no kazu

    Winter chrysanthemums!
        All along the fences
            of several cottages.

其魂の朱雀もめぐる枯野哉
sono tama no suzaku mo meguru kareno kana

    The Vermilion Bird's[223] spirit
        wanders
            the desolate fields.

---

[223] A Chinese mythological bird associated with astronomy.

身をよする冬の朝日の草のいほ

mi o yosuru fuyu no asahi no kusa no io

    I approach a grass hut
        on a sunny morning
            in winter.

はつ雪や医師に酒出す奥座敷

hatsuyuki ya ishi ni sake dasu oku zashiki

    The first snow!
        The doctor serves *sake*
            in the guest room.

犬にうつ石の扨なし冬の月

inu ni utsu ishi no sate nashi fuyu no tsuki

    There's no stone
        to throw at the dog –
            winter moon!

ゆきをみる人さわがしや夜の門
yuki o miru hito sawagashi ya yoru no mon

> Noisy people
>> snow viewing –
>>> by the gate in the evening.

医師へ行子の美しき頭巾かな
ishi e yuku ko no utsukushiki zukin kana

> The child,
>> wearing a beautiful kerchief,
>>> goes to see the doctor.

盃を持て出けり雪の中
sakazuki o mochitederu keri yuki no naka

> I took out
>> my sake cup –
>>> it's snowing all around.

壁までが板であられの山居哉

kabe made ga ita de arare no sankyo kana

> The hail
>   at this mountain retreat
>   is pounding on the wall panels.

鳴ながら狐火ともす寒かな

meinagara kitsunebi tomosu samui kana

> While birds were singing
>   in the cold,
>   a fox-fire[224] appeared.

はつ雪や町に居あはす桑門

hatsuyuki ya machi ni i awasu soumon

> The first snow!
>   I get together with a monk
>   who was in town.

---

[224] A fen-fire or will-o'-the-wisp.

末摘や炭吹おこす鼻の先
suetsumu ya sumi fuku okosu hana no saki

> The greens I gathered!
>> I blow on the charcoal to start the fire
>>> right in front of my nose.

初ゆきや酒の意趣ある人の妹
hatsuyuki ya sake no ishu aru hito no imouto

> The first snow!
>> His younger sister
>>> hates *sake*.

初霜やさすが都の竹箒
hatsushimo ya sasuga miyako no takebouki

> The first frost!
>> As expected, in the capital[225],
>>> the bamboo brooms are out.

---

[225] Kyoto.

水指のうつぶけてある寒かな

mizuyubi no utsubukete aru samui kana

Pouring out
   water from the jug –
      it's cold!

藤棚のうへからぬける落ばかな

fujidana no ue kara nukeru ochiba kana

The top
   of the wisteria trellis
      fell down.

獺に飯とられたる網代かな

kawauso ni meshi toraretaru ajiro kana

The otter
   stole its meal
      from the fishing grounds[226].

---

[226] An elaborate setup of fishing nets. A well-known one was located at Uji
   near Kyoto.

たそがれに吹おこす炭の明り哉

tasogare ni fuokosu sumi no akari kana

> At twilight
>> I blow on the charcoal
>>> whose embers start to glow.

飯喰ふて暇にしてみる冬至哉

meshi ku fute hima ni shite miru touji kana

> I see it's winter solstice
>> by the leftovers[227]
>>> as I throw them out.

花もなき水仙埋む落ばかな

hana mo naki suisen uzumu ochiba kana

> There are no more
>> daffodil blossoms –
>>> they're fallen and buried.

---

[227] Special foods were eaten on winter solstice, notably *kabocha* (squash).

225

掃けるが終には掃ず落葉かな

hakikeru ga tsui ni wa hakazu ochiba kana

> I could sweep them,
>   but in the end I don't –
>   the fallen leaves.

ぬれいろをこがらし吹や水車

nureiro o kogarashi fuku ya mizuguruma

> A cold wintry wind
>   blows on the glistening object –
>   a waterwheel[228]!

木枯や大津脚絆の店ざらし

kogarashi ya ootsukyahan no tanazarashi

> The cold winter wind!
>   For Otsu leggings[229]
>   only shopworn goods remain.

---

[228] Used for irrigation.
[229] Navy blue cotton leggings made in Otsu, now in Shiga Prefecture.

人疎し落葉のくぼむ森の道

hito utoshi rakuyou no kubomu mori no michi

> There are few people
>> on the caved-in road, covered with leaves,
>>> through the forest.

炭売よ手なら顔なら夕まぐれ

sumiuri yo te nara kao nara yuumagure

> Evening twilight becomes
>> the colour of the hands, the face,
>>> of the charcoal seller.

木がらしや手にみえ初る老が皺

kogarashi ya te ni mie hatsuru oi ga shiwa

> The cold winter wind!
>> For the first time seen on my hands,
>>> wrinkles of old age.

下戸ひとり酒に遁たる火燵哉

geko hitori sake ni nigetaru kotatsu kana

The lone non-drinker
    escapes
        to the *kotatsu*[230].

人去て暁くらき十夜かな

hito sarite akatsuki kuraki juuya kana

The people leave
    in the darkness of dawn –
        the Ten Nights service[231].

木葉散雨うちはれて夜明たり

konoha chiru ame uchi harete yoaketari

The leaves have been scattered
    by the rain –
        it clears as dawn arrives.

---

[230] A table with a futon over the frame and charcoal brazier underneath, to sit around and keep warm. This haiku seems rather like senryu (comic haiku).

[231] A ten-night service from midnight of the 6th to dawn of the 15th day of the tenth month for reciting *nembutsu* at Jodo Shinshu temples.

霜おける畠の冴へや鍬の音

shimo okeru hata no sae e ya kuwa no oto

    In the clearness
        of the frost-laden fields –
            the sound of a hoe.

つめたさに箒捨けり松の下

tsumetasa ni houki sute keri matsu no shita

    In the cold,
        I discarded the broom
            under the pine.

かみ無月旅なつかしき日ざし哉

kamimugetsu tabi natsukashiki hizashi kana

    The Godless Month[232] –
        yearning[233] to take a trip
            this sunny day.

---

[232] On the 1st day of the tenth month, all the gods left for Izumo and it was therefore called the "godless month."
[233] The idea here is that he is fondly recollecting trips of old.

229

人顔も旅の昼間や神無月

hitogao mo tabi no hiruma ya kannazuki

People's faces,
  out on a day trip –
    the Godless Month.

御築地に見こす山辺やいく時雨

otsukiji ni mi kosu yamabe ya iku shigure

Crossing over Yamabe[234]
  I see the imposing earthen walls –
    winter drizzle passing.

よるみゆる寺のたき火や冬木立

yoru miyuru tera no takibi ya fuyu kodachi

In the evening, you can see
  by the temple's bonfire
    the barren trees of winter.

---

[234] This possibly relates to a road (Yamanobe) or district near Nara.

木戸しまる音やあら井の夕千鳥
kido shimaru oto ya ara i no yuu chidori

> The sound
>   of the wicker gate closing –
>   evening plovers by the well!

一番は逃て跡なし鯨突
ichiban wa nigate ato nashi kujiratsuki

> The best ever!
>   But I lost it –
>   there's no sign of the harpooned whale.

水仙や畳の上に横たふし
suisen ya tatami no ue ni yokota fushi

> Daffodils!
>   Father and son stretched out
>   on the *tatami* mat.

水仙を生しや葉先枯る迄
suisen o nashi ya ha saki kareru made

Growing daffodils!
　　Until the tips of the leaves
　　　　start to wither.

唐へ行屏風も画やとしの暮
kara e yuku byoubu mo e ya toshi no kure

Going to China –
　　the painting on the folding screen!
　　　　New Year's Eve.

兼てよく皃見られけむ衣配
kente yoku kao mirarekemu kinukubari

Doing two things well at once –
　　noticing people's expressions
　　　　and the gift of new clothes[235] they've received.

---

[235]　Gifts of bright new clothes were presented to those close to one (usually relatives but servants too) in the twelfth lunar month for New Year's.

声よきも頼もし気也厄払

koe yoki mo tanomoshi ki nari yakubarai

> A fine voice
> > and hopeful spirit –
> > > warding off misfortune[236].

年の暮嵯峨の近道習ひけり

toshi no kure saga no chikamichi narai keri

> New Year's Eve –
> > I took the usual
> > > shortcut to Saga[237].

谷越に声かけ合ふや年木樵

tanikoshi ni koe kake au ya toshikikori

> Crossing over the valley,
> > I hear cracking sounds –
> > > cutting firewood for the new year[238].

---

236 Although there are related New Year's Eve practices (*setsubun*) this likely relates to a person who went from door to door exorcizing demons and received beans and money.

237 Formerly at the boundary of Kyoto near Arashiyama. If is near Atago Shrine, which may be the thrust of this haiku (shrine visit).

238 A December seasonal event.

宝ぶね訳の聞えぬ寐言かな
takarabune wake no kikoenu ne iu kana

The Treasure Ship[239] –
   his talking in his sleep
     is gibberish.

煤を掃く音せまり来ぬ市の中
susu o haku oto semari konu ichi no naka

In the city, the imminent sounds
   of housecleaning day[240]
     have arrived.

褌に二百くゝるや厄おとし
fundoshi ni nihyaku kukuru ya yaku otoshi

Bundling up
   two hundred loincloths –
     avoiding misfortune![241]

---

[239] A picture of a treasure ship with the Seven Gods of Good Luck and various goods was placed under one's pillow. A palindrome poem was also written on the picture. Such should bring one a lucky dream. It used to be done New Year's Eve (which applies here I believe) but is now universally done the second day of the New Year.

[240] The end of year cleaning done on the 13th day of the twelfth lunar month.

[241] This likely relates to a *hadaka matsuri* (Naked Festival) where males youth purify themselves wearing just loincloths, to ward off disease and drive out

す〻掃の埃かつぐや奈良の鹿

susuhaki no hokori katsugu ya nara no shika

> Shouldering the dust
>   from housecleaning day –
>   deer of Nara!

声立る池の家鴨やす〻払

koe ritsuru ike no ahiru ya susuharai

> Quacking loudly,
>   the domestic ducks on the pond –
>   housecleaning day!

大名に酒の友あり年忘れ

daimyou ni sake no tomo ari toshiwasure

> There are fine *sake* side dishes
>   at the *daimyo's*[242]
>   year end drinking party[243]!

---

evil spirits.
[242] A feudal lord in the Edo period.
[243] New Year's Eve drinking party to "forget" the past year.

勤行に腕の胼やうす衣
gongyou ni kaina no hibi ya usugoromo

    Praying at the temple,
        chafed arms –
            thin clothing.

鍋捨る師走の隅やくすり喰
nabe suteru shiwasu no sumi ya kusuri kuu

    Tossing out the pot into a corner
        on New Year's Eve[244] –
            taking medicine!

垣よりに若き小草や冬の雨
kaki yori ni wakaki kogusa ya fuyu no ame

    By the fence
        small young plants –
            winter rain.

---

[244]   I have interpreted "corner of the 12th month" as New Year's Eve.

氷つく芦分舟や寺の門
kouri tsuku ashiwake fune ya tera no mon

> The boat, pushing through thick reeds,
> > stuck in the ice –
> > > the temple gate.

御手洗も御灯も氷る嵐かな
mitarashi mo mitou mo kooru arashi kana

> The shrine's purifying font
> > and votive lamps too, are frozen –
> > > winter storm!

枯草に立テは落る囹かな
karekusa ni tachi te wa ochiru hitoya kana

> Standing amidst
> > the withered grass –
> > > the ruins of a prison.

父と子よよき榾くべしうれし顔

chichi to ko yo yoki hotakubeshi ureshi kao

> Father and son
> > looking forward to gather kindling –
> > > smiles of their faces!

日頃経て旨き顔なり薬ぐひ

higoro tate umaki kao nari kusuri gui

> Eating venison[245]
> > one's expression usually shows
> > > it's delicious!

寒月や留守頼れし奥の院

kangetsu ya mamori tayoreshi okunoin

> Cold winter moon!
> > Away from home,
> > > rely on the inner sanctuary[246].

---

[245]   Eating wildlife, which was not usually done, was seen as strengthening one against the rigours of winter.
[246]   This is the holiest place in a Buddhist temple or Shinto shrine: here, the Buddha or *kami* (god) within.

寒月の門へ火の飛ブ鍛冶屋哉

kangetsu no mon e hi no tobu kajiya kana

    Fire flies out the gate
        to the cold winter moon –
            the blacksmith's.

寒月や我ひとり行橋の音

kangetsu ya ware hitori yuku hashi no oto

    Cold winter moon!
        Only the sound of myself,
            crossing the bridge.

火を運ぶ旅の巨燵や夕嵐

hi o hakobu tabi no kotatsu ya yuuarashi

    On a trip,
        I bring charcoal to the *kotatsu*[247] –
            an evening tempest.

---

[247] A table with a futon over the frame and charcoal brazier underneath, to sit around and keep warm.

駕を出て寒月高し己が門

kago o dete kangetsu takashi ono ga mon

> Exiting the palanquin,
>   the winter moon
>   high above my gate.

長橋の行先かくす雪吹かな

nagahashi no ikisaki kakusu yukifu kana

> The blizzard
>   conceals the long bridge
>   that I'm headed for.

降遂ぬ雪におかしや蓑と笠

furu togenu yuki ni okashi ya mino to kasa

> It's looks weird –
>   in the never-ending snow
>   a straw raincoat and bamboo hat.

空附の竹も庇も雪吹かな
sora tsuke no take mo hisashi mo yukifu kana

> The eaves and bamboo too,
>> enclosed by the sky –
>>> a blizzard!

御次男は馬が上手で雪見かな
gojinan wa uma ga jouzude yukimi kana

> My second son
>> is good at riding a horse –
>>> going snow viewing!

宿とりて山路の吹雪覗けり
yado torite yamaji no fubuki nozo keri

> Staying at an inn,
>> I peeked out at the blizzard
>>> on the mountain road.

足つめたし目におもしろし手にか〻む

ashi tsumetashi me ni omoshiroshi te ni ka kamu

> Frozen feet,
>   blowing his nose in his hands –
>   he's some sight![248]

里へ出る鹿の背高し雪明り

sato e deru shika no sei taka shi yukiakari

> Leaving the village,
>   a large deer –
>   light reflecting off the snow.

見返るやいまは互に雪の人

mikaeru ya ima wa tagai ni yuki no hito

> Looking back at each other,
>   now we're both
>   snow men.

---

[248] This could also be self-referential.

鷹の眼や鳥によせ行袖がくれ

taka no me ya tori ni yose yuku sode ga kure

> Eyes of the falcon!
>> I bring my sleeve close –
>>> dusk.

小盃雪に埋てかくしけり

kosakazuki yuki ni uzumete kakushi keri

> The small *sake* cup
>> covered with snow –
>>> hidden!

暁の一文銭やはちたゝき

akatsuki no ichi bunsen ya hachitataki

> At dawn,
>> giving a coin –
>>> *nembutsu* dancing[249].

---

[249] *Hachitataki*: a folk performance held in winter in the Edo period where people danced, beat gongs and chanted *nembutsu* (Hail Amida Buddha), and received alms.

草の戸や巨燵の中も風の行

kusa no to ya kotatsu no naka mo kaze no yuku

> In my humble hut,
>> the wind even goes
>>> under the *kotatsu*.

淀舟やこたつの下の水の音

yodobune ya kotatsu no shita no mizu no oto

> Yodo River[250] boat –
>> under the *kotatsu*
>>> the sound of water.

今更にわたせる霜や藤の棚

imasara ni wataseru shimo ya fuji no tana

> Finally
>> the frost covers all
>>> the wisteria trellis.

---

[250]   The Yodo River runs from Lake Biwa through the Kyoto and Osaka regions.

木がらしや柴負ふ老が後より
kogarashi ya shiba ou oi ga ushiro yori

    The cold winter wind!
        An old man carrying firewood
           on his back.

恥かしやあたりゆがめし置火燵
hazukashi ya atari yugameshi okigotatsu

    It's a shame –
        the portable *kotatsu*
           was struck and bent!

行舟にこぼるゝ霜や芦の音
yuku fune ni koboreru shimo ya ashi no oto

    The boat departs –
        the sound of reeds
           covered with frost.

鶏の起けり霜のかすり声

toumaru no okoshi keri shimo no kasurigoe

    The rooster has awakened!
      In the frost
        it's call is hoarse.

初雪や旅へ遣たる従者が跡

hatsuyuki ya tabi e yaritaru juusha ga ato

    The first snow!
      Sent on an errand,
        the servant's footprints.

たのみなき若草生ふる冬田哉

tanomi naki wakakusa haeru fuyuta kana

    Nothing will help them –
      the young grasses sprouting
        in the winter rice field.

野の中に土御門家や冬至の日
no no naka ni tsuchimikadoka ya touji no hi

> The Tsuchimikados[251]
>   are in my field –
>   the winter solstice sun!

木がらしの箱根に澄や伊豆の海
kogarashi no hakone ni sumu ya izu no umi

> The winter storm over Hakone[252]
>   clears up –
>   the sea of Izu[253].

膳の時はづす遊女や納豆汁
zen no toki hazusu yuujo ya nattoujiru

> It's mealtime
>   but the courtesans slip away –
>   *natto* soup[254]!

---

251   The Tsuchimikado family were official imperial *onmyoji* – yin-yang diviners
      and "astronomers." At winter solstice yin (darkness) was at its peak and
      thereafter yang (light) would ascend and it was therefore an auspicious day.
252   A mountainous area of Kanagawa Prefecture.
253   A famous locale in Shizuoka Prefecture.
254   Miso soup with fermented soybeans. It has a very pungent odour (which I
      assume is the point here) although most Japanese like it while foreigners
      tend not to.

僧と居て古び行気や納豆汁
sou to ite furubi kouki ya nattoujiru

Staying with the old monks,
  aromatherapy[255] –
    natto soup!

人の来て言ねばしらぬ猪子哉
hito no kite iwaneba shiranu inoko kana

The person coming along,
  if I don't tell him, he won't know –
    a wild boar!

曲輪にも納豆の匂ふ斎日哉
kuruwa ni mo nattou no niou tokibi kana

The smell of natto
  in the district –
    a day of fasting[256].

---

[255] 行気 (kouki), from Chinese medicine. Taking aromatic drugs to relieve
   blocked 気, ki (Chinese, qi), vital energy flowing through our bodies.
[256] A Buddhist day, fasting from noon to dawn. Many people are getting their
   fill of natto in the morning.

雪やつむ障子の所の音更ぬ
yuki ya tsumu shouji no kami no oto kou nu

Snow piling up!
　　Through the paper *shoji,*
　　　　the hour strikes[257].

立波に足みせて行ちどりかな
tatsunami ni ashi misete yuku chidori kana

Plovers can be seen
　　running
　　　　in the rolling waves.

大食のむかしがたりや鰤の前
taishoku no mukashigatari ya buri no mae

Tales of long ago
　　about gluttony –
　　　　before me a yellowtail fish.

---

[257] Actually every second hour. In the evening a watchman made his rounds sounding off the time. Each 2 hour period had a set number of "strokes." The night had five such periods.

身を守る尖ともみえぬ海鼠哉

mi o mamoru togatomo mienu namako kana

> Protecting its body
>> the sea cucumber ejects filaments
>>> and can't be seen[258].

胴切にしもせざりける海鼠かな

dougiri ni shi mo sezari keru namako kana

> Cutting it in half,
>> it's not yet dead –
>>> the sea cucumber.

鴨の毛を捨るも元の流かな

kamo no ke o suteru mo moto no nagare kana

> The discarded
>> duck feathers
>>> float away.

---

[258] The filaments are sticky and are for entangling a predator, rather than hiding the sea cucumber. However, an observer might think it is hiding itself.

ちどり啼暁もどる女かな

chidori naku akatsuki modoru onna kana

> A dawn
>   the plovers cry
>   as the women return[259].

菊好や切らで枯行花の数

kikuzuki ya setsura de kareyu hana no kazu

> Chrysanthemum lover!
>   Cutting a number
>   of withered blossoms.

口切のとまり客あり峰の坊

kuchikiri no tomari kyaku ari mine no bou

> The guests staying overnight,
>   opening a jar of tea[260] –
>   mountain monastery.

---

[259] These may be *ama*, women divers (for seafood in the Edo), or fisherwomen in general.

[260] A jar of new summer tea is opened at the beginning of the tenth lunar month.

草の屋の行灯もとぼす火桶哉
kusa no ya no andon mo tobosu hioke kana

    Using the wooden brazier
        to light the paper lantern
           of the thatched shop.

塩鱈や旅はるばるのよごれ面
shiotara ya tabi harubaru no yogore tsura

    Salted cod!
        All dirty
           after the long journey.

頭巾脱でいたゞくやこのぬくい物
zukin datsu de itadaku ya kono nukui mono

    Receiving the hood
        that's taken off –
           it's warm!

頭巾おく袂や老のひが覚へ
zukin oku tamoto ya oi no hi ga oboe

    I put the hood
        in my sleeve –
            the failing memory of an old man.

帰来て夜をねぬ音や池の鴛
kaerikite yo o nenu oto ya ike no oshi

    Evening returns
        Not yet sleeping, sounds –
            mandarin ducks on the pond.

意趣のある狐見延す枯野かな
ishu no aru kitsune mimawasu kareno kana

    The fox
        maliciously surveys
            the desolate field.

河豚喰し人の寐言の念仏かな

fugu kuishi hito no negoto no nenbutsu kana

Having eaten blowfish[261],
   the man in his sleep
      recites the *nembutsu*[262].

塀越の枯野やけふの魂祭

heigoshi no kareno ya kyou no tamamatsuri

Crossing the fence
   of a desolate field –
      Festival of the Dead[263] today.

死ぬやうにひとは言也ふくと汁

shinu ya u ni hito wa ii nari fukutojiru

I'm dying!
   says the man still living –
      blowfish soup.

---

[261] If not cleaned properly, eating this fish can be fatal.
[262] "Hail to Amida Buddha." Recited to ensure birth in the Pure Land.
[263] Tama Matsuri, another appellation for Obon Matsuri (Festival), when spirits return to their birthplace. Literally, "soul festival." The season word is "desolate field" (winter). There is feel of Tama Matsuri but it is not that day.

鰒喰ふて酒呑下戸のおもひかな
fugu kuite sakenomi geko no omoi kana

    Eating blowfish,
        I think of heavy drinkers
            and non-drinkers.

夜明ぬとふとん剥けり旅の友
yoakenu to futon hagu keri tabi no tomo

    Not yet dawn,
        I fold up the futon –
            journey to a friend's.

旅の身に添や鋪寐の駕ぶとん
tabi no mi ni soe ya shiki ne no kagobuton

    Just right for my trip –
        the palanquin futon
            for sleeping.

鰒売に喰ふべき顔とみられけり

fugu uri ni kuubeki kao to mirare keri

    The blowfish seller's face
        looks like
            he's eaten some.

人ごゝろ幾度河豚を洗ひけむ

hitogokoro ikudo fukube o araikemu

    I guess it's human nature
        to wash the blowfish
            so many times!

帋子着てはるばる来たり寺林

kamiko kite harubaru kitari terabayashi

    Coming from the distant
        temple woods
            wearing a paper robe[264].

---

[264]   A thin outer garment worn in winter to protect against the wind.

活僧の蒲団をた〻む魔風哉
kassou no futon o tatamu makaze kana

    An evil spirit's wind
        folds up the futon
            of the holy monk.

足が出て夢も短かき蒲団かな
ashi ga dete yume mo mijikaki futon kana

    My feet are sticking out –
        again I dream
            my futon is too short.

わびしさや旅寐の蒲団数をよむ
wabishisa ya tabine no futon kazu o yomu

    Loneliness –
        lying in bed on a trip
            counting off futons.

それぞれの星あらはるゝさむさ哉

sorezore no hoshi arawareru samusa kana

> All the stars
>   are out –
>   the cold!

紙子着しおとや夜舟の隅の方

kamiko ki shi oto ya yobune no sumi no kata

> The sound of wearing a paper robe[265] –
>   the prow of a boat
>   in the evening.

僧にする子を膝もとや冬ごもり

sou ni suru ko o hizamoto ya fuyugomori[266]

> The child becoming a monk
>   clasps his mother's legs[267] –
>   staying indoors.

---

[265] A thin outer garment worn in winter to protect against the wind.
[266] A winter event. It's too cold to go outside.
[267] The original does not explicitly state who it is.

いつまでも女嫌ひぞ冬籠
itsumademo onnagirai zo fuyugomori

Forever
     a misogynist –
          staying indoors.

冬ごもり古き揚屋に訊れけり
fuyugomori furuki ageya ni kikare keri

Staying indoors –
     I heard sounds
          coming from the old brothel.

おどらせぬむすめ連行十夜哉
odorasenu musume renkou juuya kana

They don't let their daughter dance –
     they're dragging her off
          to the Ten Nights service[268].

---

[268] A ten-night service from midnight of the 6th to dawn of the 15th day of the tenth month for reciting nembutsu at Jodo Shinshu temples.

達磨忌や宗旨代々不信心

darumaki ya shuushi daidai fushinjin

Daruma's memorial[269] –
generation after generation
the sect of impiety[270].

あら笑止十夜に落る庵の根太

ara shoushi juuya ni ochiru io no nebuto

Ah, it's absurd –
during Ten Nights service
a joist at the hermitage fell down.

夜歩行の子に門で逢ふ十夜かな

yoru hokou no ko ni kado de au juuya kana

By the gate, I meet a child
walking in the evening –
the Ten Nights service.

---

[269] Bodhidharma, semi-legendary founder of Chan (Zen) Buddhism in the early 5th century. His memorial in Japan is the 5th day of the tenth month.
[270] I presume this refers to Zen's iconoclastic ways. "Sect" here could also be "doctrine." Taigi was a Zen monk for a time.

米搗の所を替る落葉哉

kometsuki no tokoro o kawaru ochiba kana

> The place I go
>> to relieve the man pounding rice –
>>> fallen leaves.

炉開や世に遁たる夫婦合

robiraki ya yo ni nogaretaru meotoai

> Opening the winter hearth!
>> Escaping the world –
>>> husband and wife.

川澄や落葉の上の水五寸

kawasumi ya ochiba no ue no mizu go sun

> The clear river –
>> six inches[271] of water
>>> above the fallen leaves.

---

[271] Five *sun* (one *sun* = 1.2 inches).

盗人に鐘つく寺や冬木立
nusubito ni kane tsuku tera ya fuyukodachi

> The temple bell tolls
>> upon the thief –
>>> the barren trees of winter.

麦蒔や声で鴈追ふ片手業
mugimaki ya koe de gan ou katatewaza

> Planting barley!
>> The cry of the geese scared off –
>>> winter chores.

中窪き径わび行落葉かな
nakakuboki wataru wabi yuku ochiba kana

> In the trough
>> a desolate row
>>> of fallen leaves.

冬枯や雀のありく戸樋の中

fuyugare ya suzume no ariku toi no naka

> Winter desolation –
> > sparrows hopping about
> > > in the rain gutters.

濡にける的矢をしはくしぐれ哉

nure ni keru matoya o shi haku shigure kana

> Getting wet
> > so I gather up the target and arrows –
> > > winter drizzle.

玄関にて御傘と申時雨哉

genkan ni te gosan to mou shigure kana

> In the entranceway I call
> > for the "honourable umbrella[272]" –
> > > winter drizzle.

---

[272] *"Gosan"* is also the name of a famous haiku reference work by Sadanori Matsunaga (1571–1654).

うぐひすのしのび歩行や夕時雨

uguisu no shinobi hokou ya yuushigure

Out walking,
    the bush warbler is hidden –
        evening drizzle[273].

しらで猶余所に聞なす水鶏かな

shira de nao yoso ni kikunasu kuina kana

I know of another instance
    of one sounding human[274] –
        the water rail!

剃こかす若衆のもめや年の暮

sorikokasu wakashu no mome ya toshi no kure

A quarrel over
    shaving[275] the youth's head –
        end of the year.

---

[273] This haiku has two season terms "bush warbler" (spring) and "evening rain" (winter). It was grouped with other winter haiku.

[274] Usually this relates to a bird's call sounding like Japanese words but here it has a broader meaning. The water rail was known to make a tapping sound like a knock at the door. This motif was common in haiku (e.g Basho).

[275] This would be full shaving to enter the Buddhist order rather than coming of age.

www.ingramcontent.com/pod-product-compliance
Lightning Source LLC
LaVergne TN
LVHW051113080426
835510LV00018B/2016